Fly Fish Virginia

A No Nonsense Guide to Top Waters

Beau Beasley

Foreword by King Montgomery

Picturesque North Creek. Photo by Beau Beasley.

NO NONSENSE

**Fly Fishing
Virginia**

A No Nonsense Guide to Top Waters
ISBN-10 1-892469-16-2
ISBN-13 978-1-892469-16-8

© 2007 Beau Beasley

Published by:
No Nonsense Fly Fishing Guidebooks
P.O. Box 91858
Tucson, AZ 85752-1858
(520) 547-2462
www.nononsenseguides.com
2 3 4 5 6   12 11 10 09
Printed in China

Editors: Howard Fisher, Caroline Pederson

Maps, Illustrations, Design & Production:
Pete Chadwell, Dynamic Arts; Doug
Goewey

About the Cover
Front—Tom Brown fishing the lower
Jackson River. Photo by Beau Beasley.

Back—Although Beau Beasley will fish for
nearly anything that swims, this day he
settled for a nice rainbow trout. Photo by
Larry Coburn.

Dedication

This book is dedicated to my wonderful wife Leila McLaurin Beasley, the most important and best catch of my life. Your encouragement and editing are what brought about this book.

Acknowledgments

When I set out to write *Fly Fishing Virginia*, I thought it would be a simple project. I quickly learned that I would not be able to write this book alone. Along the way I had a lot of encouragement and assistance. First, I owe the most thanks to my wonderful wife Leila who edited every word of this book and read and reread the manuscript many times.

I am also greatly indebted to my good friend and mentor King Montgomery, who helped out a great deal with photography and has always encouraged my writing. Thanks also to C. Boyd Pfeiffer and Lefty Kreh for their words of advice about how to write a book. Lee Walker and Larry Mohn with the Virginia Department of Game and Inland Fisheries also gave me some great advice about what to cover. Most Virginians have no idea how hard this agency works for its sportsmen.

Many thanks to the folks at *Fly Fish America*, who gave me my first national writing platform. To the many guides and shop owners who assisted me, space constraints prevent me from listing each of you individually—but you know who you are, and I thank you. And I would be remiss if I did not mention the hard work of Howard Fisher, Doug Goewey, and the other fine folks at No Nonsense Fly Fishing Guidebooks, and map creator, photographer and designer Pete Chadwell of Dynamic Arts.

I would also especially like to recognize John Ross, Paul Kearney, Dan Genest and Captain Cory Routh for their technical assistance and advice. Last but not least, I wish to thank John Loss, a firefighter's firefighter, who knew that I would write this book before I did. Thanks, John. You have no idea how much you really helped.

My introduction to fishing came from my father, the hardest-working man I've ever known. Although he routinely worked long hours and often traveled several hundred miles away from our humble home in South Hill, Virginia, in pursuit of work, he made time to take me fishing. I still remember him loading me and my little brother Jason and all of our gear into his old blue pickup truck. My loving mother, a newspaper reporter at the time, knew how important this family time was and sometimes joined us on our fishing excursions.

Years before I became a fly fisherman, I remember my father casting to resident bluegill and the occasional bass in a nearby farm pond. Looking back, my fondest childhood memories are of the times I spent fishing with my Daddy.

It is my sincere hope that you enjoy using this book as much as I've enjoyed writing it. I also hope that if given the opportunity, you take your own children fishing with you. Those memories may last a lifetime.

—Beau Beasley

The author on the Rose River. Photo by Tim Esau.

About the Author

Beau Beasley is just as likely to chase smallies on the New River as he is to track brook trout in the cold mountain streams of the Old Dominion. His father introduced him to farm pond fishing as a child, but he's equally happy to pursue stripers in the Chesapeake Bay or follow the early spring shad migrations across Virginia, fly rod in hand.

Beau began writing in the mid 1990s and has been published in *Fly Fisherman, Fly Rod & Reel, American Angler, Mid-Atlantic Fly Fishing Guide, Virginia Wildlife, Flyfisher, Fly Tyer, Chesapeake Angler, Richmond Magazine, Virginia Living,* and *Virginia Sportsman.* He is a contributing editor for *Fly Fish America* and the Mid-Atlantic field editor for *Eastern Fly Fishing.*

In addition to writing, Beau is the director of the annual Virginia Fly Fishing Festival and is a 25-year veteran career captain with Fairfax County Fire and Rescue Department assigned to Engine Company 427. His first book, *Fly Fishing Virginia: A No Nonsense Guide to Top Waters,* was released in May 2007 and is in bookstores throughout the country. He lives with his wife and children in Warrenton, Virginia.

To learn more about Beau or his book, visit his Web site at www.beaubeasley.com, or contact your local fly shop.

Table of Contents

Photo by King Montgomery.

Photo by Beau Beasley.

Photo by Beau Beasley.

Photo by Eric Evans.

Photo by Beau Beasley.

Photo by Beau Beasley.

Photo by Chris Newsome.

Natural Bridge near North Creek.
Photo courtesy of the Virginia Tourism Corporation.

Foreword

The first things I noticed about Beau Beasley when he introduced himself to me almost 15 years ago were his firm handshake and sincere eye contact when he spoke and listened. It was at a small fishing show in Fairfax County, and this young fireman/paramedic clutched several popper bodies in his other hand. He asked what I thought about the closed-cell foam bodies, and I told him they seemed a little heavy, but I'd be glad to give them a try once they were tied.

Beau has fished most of his life while growing up in the Old Dominion, but it was these poppers, designed by a fine Virginia gentleman by the name of Bob Guess, that introduced him to the world of fly fishing. Mr. Bob's Poppers soon became my go-to popper/slider for largemouth and smallmouth bass and for sunfishes when they were tied in the smaller sizes. Beau actively marketed the poppers, which did well for several years until the popper body supplier priced himself out of contention in a competitive world. I still have some Mr. Bob's Poppers and still hook a lot of bass with them. And, most important, they helped Beau Beasley get hooked on fly fishing.

Beau became an enthusiastic student and practitioner of fly fishing and quickly established a solid reputation in the fly angling community. He worked as a tackle representative for several fly fishing companies and traveled around the state selling their wares while sampling the many waters Virginia has to offer. He successfully promoted The Old Dominion Fly Fishing Show and eventually sold it. He is the director of the popular Virginia Fly Fishing Festival in Waynesboro, and is active in conservation efforts throughout the state. And with my support and encouragement—Beau is a born story-teller—he became a fine outdoor writer and photographer with credits in many national, regional and state publications.

In this, his first, book, Beau shares with us some of his favorite waters in the Commonwealth including trout streams, bass haunts, and saltwater spots. We are blessed with an abundance of trout streams, almost 3,000 miles of them, from rivers to small mountain brooks. Our bass lakes, reservoirs, ponds and rivers provide some of the best largemouth and smallmouth fishing in the nation. And the Virginia waters of the Chesapeake Bay and its rivers are home to a variety of desirable game fishes such as striped bass, bluefish, various sea trouts, and others.

Fly Fishing Virginia: A No Nonsense Guide to Top Waters is nicely written and photographed and well-researched by its author. The maps are invaluable, and Beau has checked each one on the ground and on the water. Follow these maps from where you are to where you want to be, and once at the chosen location, tie on one of the flies that Beau recommends. Many of the flies noted in the guide are Virginia originals and proven fish-catchers.

Thanks to Beau's diligence and ability to communicate clearly and concisely, this guide book puts you onto some of the finest fly fishing in the Old Dominion. Beau has accomplished all the hard work. All you need to do is follow his lead, and catch (and release) fish.

—King Montgomery
Outdoor Writer/Photographer
Burke, Virginia

Fly Fishing Virginia

I had one simple goal in mind in writing *Fly Fishing Virginia*: I wanted to write a book that the average fly angler could learn from and use right away. I also wanted the maps to be readable, sensible, and accurate. I wanted the chapters about each river to be helpful as well as interesting. I wanted the fly selections to be clear and also innovative. In short, I wanted the regular angler—the guy or gal just like me—to be able to pick up this book and, with little or no additional assistance, stand a reasonably good chance of having a successful day on the water.

In pursuit of that goal, I have spent a great deal of time researching Virginia waters and uncovering unique local patterns. But don't cry for me—I've enjoyed every minute of this "research." In addition, I have had a great deal of assistance from top-notch guides and fly shop owners across the Old Dominion as well as from the experts at the Virginia Department of Game and Inland Fisheries. Of course, no book is perfect, least of all mine, and I take full responsibility for any mistakes found on these pages.

How to Use This Book

I wrote this book for all fly anglers, from novice to veteran. Each section has an overview of a particular water, usually including some history of the surrounding area. In addition, you will find gear selections, fly recommendations, and a general idea of what should be hatching or what baitfish are in the area. Each water features a map with areas of interest noted. While these maps are just a thumbnail sketch of how to get to the water, they should be more than enough to get you pointed in the right direction.

Catch and Release

Though I see nothing wrong with bringing a few fish home to eat every now and then, I am a strong proponent of catch and release fly fishing. In my opinion the only thing better than catching a nice fish is releasing it with the hope of catching it again one day.

Rules and Regulations

Educate yourself about the game laws and limits for the areas that you plan to fish, including the regulations associated with special trout waters and delayed harvesting. For the latest in game laws and creel limits, check out the website of the Virginia Department of Game and Inland Fisheries (VDGIF) at www.dgif.state.va.us.

Virginia has a lot to offer saltwater fly anglers as well. There is a whole host of species for those that want to pursue fish in the Chesapeake Bay and its surrounding tributaries. To keep abreast of saltwater regulations, check out the recreational fishing section on the Virginia Marine Resources Commission's website at www.mrc.virginia.gov.

Conservation

In terms of conserving our scarce and fragile natural resources, anglers make a choice every time they head to the water: will I be part of the solution today, or will I be part of the problem? To leave a safe, sustainable planet to those who come behind us, we must ourselves practice—and instill in those over whom we have some influence—a lifestyle of responsible resource management. Do your part, whether that means adhering to game laws or picking up someone else's streamside trash.

Hazards and Safety

Most of what you can do to ensure a safe day on the water is just good common sense. First, drink plenty of water to prevent dehydration. Remember your prescription medicine if you're going on an extended trip. Let others know where you are going and when you should return. Take along a raincoat, sunglasses, and an extra pair of clothes.

As a firefighter and medic I have responded to thousands of emergency calls for help. So often, alcohol or drug use is involved. Please consider forgoing that alcoholic libation while on the water. You'll have plenty of time to celebrate your successful day when you get home. Wading or boating while drinking alcohol is a recipe for disaster.

If you fish from a boat, make certain that you and your guests are familiar with all of the onboard safety features. In the fall of 2006 I did some "research" on the Chesapeake Bay with Captain Tony Harding of Latitude Charters. As I leaned over to untangle my fly from the bow line, a rogue wave hit the back of the boat and flipped me head over heels into the Bay. Bobbing in 52-degree water up to my armpits was not a pleasant experience. Captain Harding reacted swiftly and with the calm reserve for which he is well known. Within a matter of moments, he had fished me out of the water with a life ring and we were headed back to the dock. In the end we all had a good laugh. Had I not kept my cool, however, and had he not been prepared for emergencies, the day might have ended tragically rather than with a funny story.

An inviting pool at Whitetop Laurel Creek. Photo by Beau Beasley.

Rods

Rods are categorized by weights. The smaller the number, the lighter and often shorter the rod—and usually the game fish being pursued. For example, trout rod weights run 0 to 5 and are often 7½ to 8 or 9 feet in length. Most bass rods are 6 to 8 weights and are generally 9 feet in length. Saltwater rods range from 8 to 15 weights and generally run from 9 to 10½ feet in length. To find the rod that is right for you, contact your local fly shop.

Reels

Fly reels are sized like rods: the smaller the reel, the smaller the rod with which it will be compatible. Fresh water anglers—who use reels primarily to hold line and not to stop fish—can get by with a simple click and pawl reel. Saltwater reels are a horse of a different color. Some saltwater reels with serious stopping power are designed with disc drags that could stop the forward progress of your first car. Take your time when selecting your reel to ensure that it is the best fit for your rod.

Lines and Leaders

The three most common fly lines are weight-forward floating, intermediate-sinking, and fast-sinking. Most trout fishermen use a weight-forward floating line, preferred for casting surface flies. Anglers use intermediate lines for some fresh water applications and frequently for saltwater fishing. Sinking lines generally come in grain weights ranging from 150 to 700. Tungsten is the primary product used in sinking lines; the higher the grain weight, the heavier the line. Not all lines can be used on all rods, so check with your fly shop if you're unsure.

Fly Patterns

This book highlights the works of some of Virginia's best fly tyers, including Dusty Wissmath, Harrison Steeves, Tommy Mattioli, Brian Trow, Blane Chocklett, and Chuck Kraft. I am particularly proud to cast a spotlight on popper legend Walt Cary, who at the printing of this book will have been making popping bugs in the Old Dominion for 50 years!

I hope that readers are as thrilled with the color photos of recommended patterns as I am. Among the myriad Virginia patterns listed, you will also find Coburn's Cress Bug, Jay's Patuxent Special, and DuBiel's Red-Ducer. True, these patterns originate from Maryland and North Carolina. Virginia fish, however, don't seem to know that these flies weren't created for them, and I'm not about to tell them.

Wading Gear

Wading is one of the great joys of angling. Even anglers who use kayaks and other personal floatation devices like pontoon boats often use them to get better wading access. The three most common forms of wading are wet wading, using hip boots, and using chest waders. Wet wading means getting in the water in your shorts or swimsuit, with wading boots, and it's my favorite way to fish. Hip boots are about ¾ of the length of your legs and are perfect for small stream fishing in places like the Shenandoah National Park (and for brook trout fishing in particular). Finally, anglers may opt for waders that cover all the way to one's chest. Whichever method you choose, make sure you use felt-soled boots. No other sole is as reliable when it comes to keeping your footing.

Remain alert and aware when you are wading. Each year anglers die wading because they are too complacent or overconfident in their ability. Rivers are beautiful—they can also be powerful and deadly. Remember that, and live to fish another day.

Guides

Are you hitting a particular water for the first time? Hiring a guide is almost always a wise investment. Guides are the resident experts of the water and may spend as many as 250 days a year fishing it. And please—if you choose to hire a guide, listen to what he or she tells you to do.

You will find a listing of guides for fresh and saltwater in the resource section of this book. I have tried to compile as complete a list as possible, but I undoubtedly missed some folks. If you know a guide who is not listed here, this is not necessarily a reflection on his or her skill or professionalism. More likely, it

Keep a low profile while trout fishing.
Photo by Beau Beasley.

simply means that I don't know him or her. Having said that, guides are like rivers: some are indeed better than others. You won't go wrong calling around to fly shops and doing your homework before hiring a guide.

Fly Shops

The local fly shop is your best source for the skinny you need on the water you want to fish. In this Internet age, independent fly shops are having trouble making ends meet. If you want to keep that crucial wealth of information available to you and to the rest of us, please do your part: visit the local fly shop for tips and information, and then consider picking up local patterns and maybe even a complete outfit (when you're again in the market for one) from the shop owners who do right by you.

Private Fishing Waters

Public streams can sometimes get crowded. To improve your odds on the water, you might consider a fee-for-fishing trip on a private stream that is managed by professionals. I have listed four fee-for-fishing waters in this book. I recommend them all without reservation.

Ratings

Each river in the book is rated on a 1 to 10 scale (poor to excellent) and as you might expect, these ratings are completely subjective. I have tried to consider the species available, access, scenery, and the length of the season on that water. Indeed, I might view a good or bad fishing experience very differently from many readers. I believe that I have covered most of the prime waters in the state (and made a few off-the-beaten-path recommendations), yet Virginia boasts numerous gems that I haven't covered here.

Clubs and Organizations

Consider joining an organization that promotes fly angling and waterway conservation. I wholeheartedly endorse groups like Trout Unlimited, The Federation of Fly Fishers, and the Coastal Conservation Association. I am also a huge fan of the Chesapeake Bay Foundation and would suggest that if you have a few extra bucks lying around, these folks will put your donation to good use.

Keep an open mind toward your fellow outdoor sportsmen. Though clubs such as the Potomac River Smallmouth Club may include spin fishermen, trust me: these guys know a thing or two about fishing and can save you a lot of time and effort by giving you some great tips. Fly anglers are not the only folks who know how to read the water and find fish. Remember that the only thing better than going fishing is going fishing with a friend.

Standard Trout Flies—Dries

Adams Parachute

Blue Winged Olive

Black Fur Ant

Braided Butt Damsel

Dave's Cricket

Elk Hair Caddis

Black Foam Flying Ant

Light Hendrickson

Whitlock's Hopper

Humpy

Light Cahill

Yellow Sally

Madam X

March Brown

Pale Morning Dun

Quill Gordon

Royal Wulff

Stimulator (Yellow)

Standard Trout Flies—
Nymphs and Streamers

Beadhead Goldilox

Copper Johns

Green Weenie

Beadhead Hare's Ear Nymph

Matuka (Olive)

Mickey Finn

Muddler Minnow

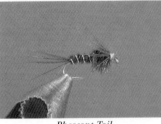
Pheasant Tail

Beadhead Pheasant Tail

Beadhead Prince Nymph

River Witch

RS2

San Juan Worm

Stonefly Nymph

Scud

Sculpin

Woolly Bugger

Zug Bug

Standard Bass Flies &
Standard Saltwater Patterns

Big Nasty Crayfish

Clouser Minnow

Dahlberg Diver

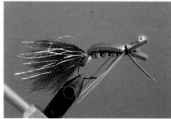
Hansen's Electric Frog

MC2 Crayfish

Mohnsen's Buggit

San Antonio Worm

Shenk's White Minnow

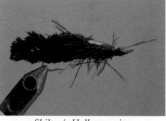
Skilton's Hellgrammite

Zonker

Blanton's Flashtail Whistler

Bruce's Bay Anchovie

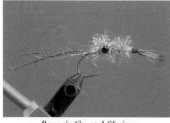
Bruce's Crystal Shrimp

Crazy Charlie

Lefty's Deceiver

Lefty's Half and Half

Simmons' Shad Fly

Trow's Minnow Saltwater

Virginia Specialty Flies—
Trout, Bass, and Saltwater

Bruce's Little Bow

Coburn's Cress Bug

Coburn's Inchworm

Dover's Peach Fly

Dusty's Deviant

Finn's Golden Retriever

Gelso's Little Black Stonefly

Murray's Mr. Rapidan

Steeves' Attract Ant

Steeves' Bark Beetle

Steeves' Crystal Butt Hopper

Steeves' Disc O' Beetle

Steeves' UFO

Chocklett's Disc Slider

Claw-Dad

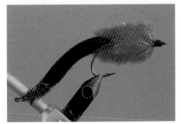
Cramer's Jail Bait Minnow

Hickey's Condor (Orange)

Kreelex

14

Murray's Lead Eye Hellgrammite

Murray's Marauder

Patuxent Special

Super Patuxent Special

Trow's Minnow

Walt's Popper

Walt's Slider

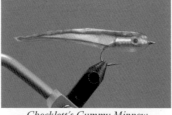
Chocklett's Gummy Minnow

CK Baitfish

DuBiel's Finesse Fly

DuBiel's Lil'hadden

DuBiel's Red-Ducer

Russell's Mussel

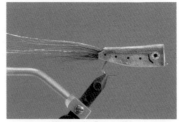
Tommy's Crease Fly

Tommy's Eel Fly

Tommy's Torpedo (Chartreuse)

Tommy's Flash Torpedo (Orange)

Walt's Saltwater Popper

Shawn Hamilton of Eastern Fly Fishing *magazine with a nice New River smallie. Photo by Beau Beasley.*

Top Virginia Fly Fishing Waters

Natural Chimneys

PASSAGE CREEK
SPECIAL REGULATION AREA

OCTOBER 1 THROUGH MAY 31:
ARTIFICIAL LURE WITH SINGLE HOOK ONLY PERMITTED
ALL TROUT MUST BE RELEASED UNHARMED
NO TROUT OR BAIT MAY BE IN POSSESSION WHILE FISHING

JUNE 1 TO SEPTEMBER 30:
GENERAL STATEWIDE TROUT REGULATIONS APPLY

OCTOBER 1 TO JUNE 15:
TROUT LICENSE REQUIRED IN ADDITION TO FISHING LICENSE

Lower Jackson

Passage Creek

All photos by Beau Beasley.

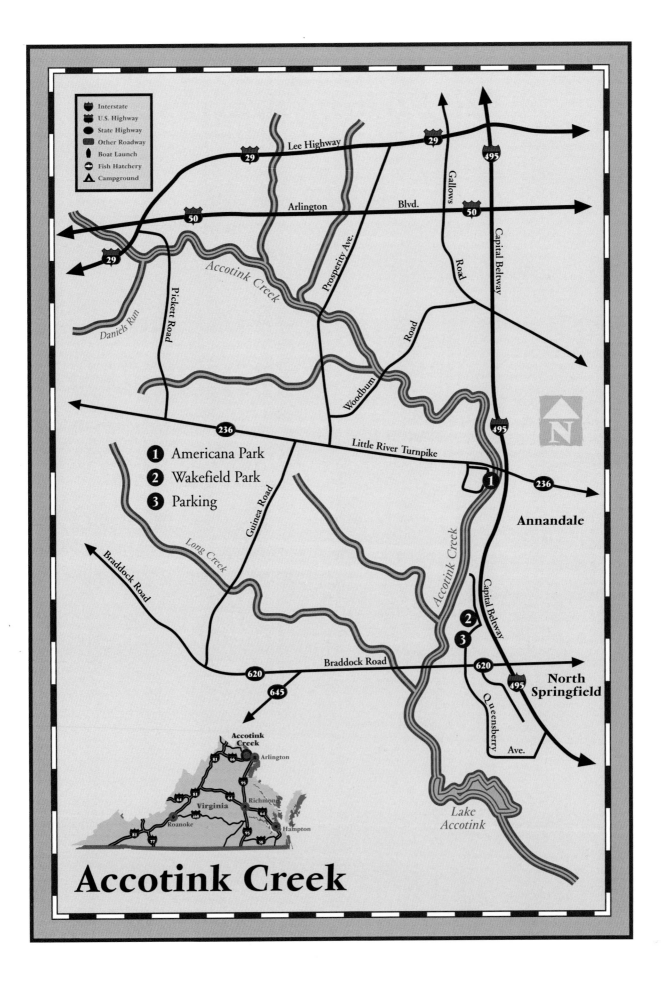

Accotink Creek

1 Americana Park
2 Wakefield Park
3 Parking

Accotink Creek

If you listen carefully you can probably hear the traffic of Northern Virginia whizzing by you as you stand fishing in Accotink Creek. But why listen? Yes, you can actually see Accotink Creek when exiting onto Little River Turnpike from the Capital Beltway. Yes, each day tens of thousands of people slog their way to and from work mere paces from an urban trout stream and they don't even realize it. But here's the thing: if you're fishing in Accotink Creek, then you are not, at least for the day, one of those poor sods. Enjoy it. Don't listen for the traffic.

While no one will argue that this is trout fishing at its best, Accotink Creek has been a godsend for a lot of folks who just needed to get away for a few hours and feel the tug of a trout. It's stocked by the game department a few times each year with the help of the Northern Virginia Chapter of Trout Unlimited. I have also been there to help and have watched as the stocking truck doled out happy rainbows in the 12-inch range. TU volunteers then scurried over embankments and soft sand to deposit their treasures in the waiting waters. In the winter, TU members have had to break the ice with shovels in some places of the creek to make a comfortable place to deposit the fish.

Accotink Creek is a classic example of doing the best you can with what you have. Although it's certainly light years from fishing in the Shenandoah National Park or a great trout water like the Jackson River, it beats not fishing at all. Accotink Creek has easy access from both Little River Turnpike and Braddock Road and is certainly worth a look. Besides, you might decide that you need a day away from the office when you're already on your way to work. Think of it: you can pull over and trout fish until the traffic lightens up enough to go home.

Burt Weisman, a member of the Northern Virginia Chapter of TU, during a fall stocking. Photo by Beau Beasley.

Types of Fish
Rainbow trout, brown trout.

Known Hatches
Hendrickson, March Brown, Little Yellow Stonefly, Sulfur, Caddis, Cahill, inchworm, terrestrials.

Equipment to Use
Rods: 4-6 weight, 7½ to 8 feet.
Reels: Mechanical and palm.
Lines: Weight forward floating matched to rod.
Leaders: 4X-5X leaders 9 feet in length.
Wading: Hip waders are fine here.

Flies to Use
Dries: Adams #14-20, BWO #14-20, Braided Butt Damsel #10-12, Dusty's Deviant #12-16, Elk Hair Caddis #14-20, Flying Ant #10-18, Gelso's Little Black Stonefly #16-20, Lt. Cahill #14-20, Little Yellow Sally #14-20, March Brown #10-14, Murray's Mr. Rapidan #14-20, Pale Morning Dun #14-20, Quill Gordon #12-22, Stimulator #12-20, Steeves' Attract Ant #16-20, Steeves' Bark Beetle #16-20, Steeves' Crystal Butt Hopper #8-10, Steeves' Disc O' Beetle #14, Steeves' UFO #10. *Nymphs & Streamers:* BH Goldilox #6-10, BH Hare's Ear #14-20, BH Prince Nymph #14-20, Bruce's Little Bow #6, Coburn's Cress Bug #14-20, Coburn's Inchworm #12-14, Egg #6-20, Finn's Golden Retriever #6-10, Green Weenie #14-16, Matuka #4-10, Mickey Finn #6-10, MC2 Crayfish #4-6, Muddler Minnow #6-10, Pheasant Tail #14-20, River Witch #6, Scud #10-18, Sculpin #4-8, Woolly Bugger #6-10.

When to Fish
Fishing is best here from March to November. It's a good idea to avoid Accotink Creek in July and August due to low water flows.

Season & Limits
Open all year. A delayed–harvest area exists here for nearly two miles. From October 1 through the following May 31, only artificial lures may be used, and all fish must be released. From June through September, general trout regulations apply. A trout license is required to fish here.

Nearby Fly Fishing
Holmes Run is a local alternative.

Accommodations & Services
There are abundant services nearby in Annandale.

Rating
Though certainly not what one might call picturesque trout fishing, Accotink's location makes it accessible to those who need a fishing fix but can't make the trek to more remote waters. Accotink Creek rates an easy 6.

Catch brown trout just minutes from bumper-to-bumper traffic. Photo by King Montgomery.

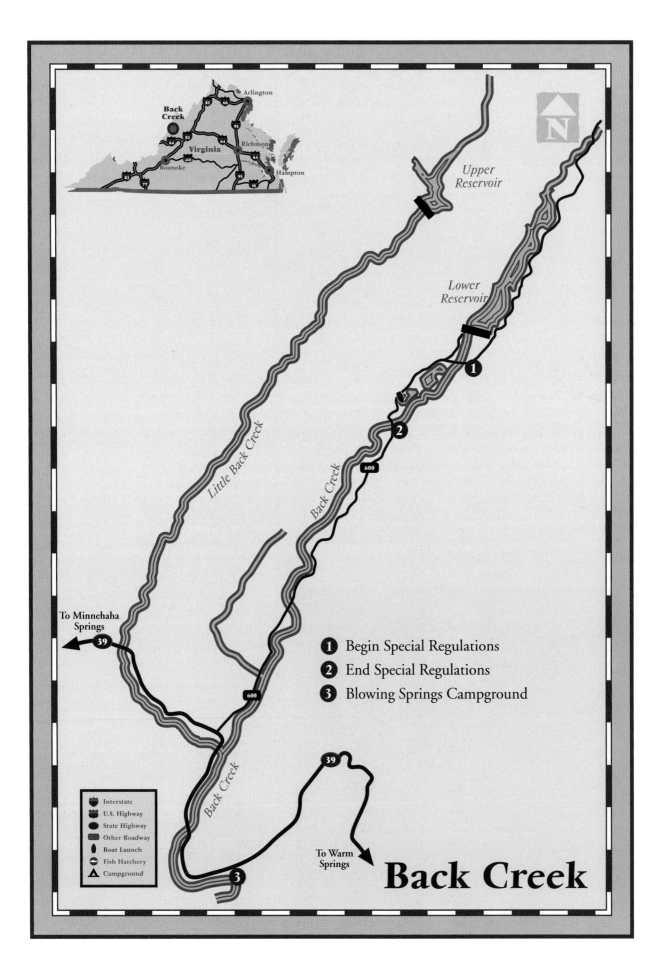

Upper
Reservoir

Lower
Reservoir

Little Back Creek

Back Creek

1 Begin Special Regulations
2 End Special Regulations
3 Blowing Springs Campground

To Minnehaha
Springs

To Warm
Springs

Back Creek

Interstate
U.S. Highway
State Highway
Other Roadway
Boat Launch
Fish Hatchery
Campground

Back Creek

Back Creek

Back Creek, tucked away in the far western reaches of the state, is home to beautiful rainbows and browns—and some of the most breathtaking scenery imaginable. This outlying area was the military training ground of a young colonel in the Virginia Militia named George Washington. Then only in his early 20s, Washington, tasked with devising a way to protect vulnerable settlers from the American Indians of Virginia and Ohio, came up with the idea of stringing forts along the outer edges of the state in a defensive position. This approach worked and provided security for the local civilian population.

It was here that Washington also witnessed brutal close quarters combat fighting alongside the British Army. In a battle near the Monongahela National Forest, Washington witnessed something that he would remember all his life: Indians scored a military victory over the British and forced them and the Virginia Militia to a draw. It was here, then, that Washington first realized that the British Army was not the unbeatable force that he, a loyal British subject, had always believed it to be. He would recall this incident years later as Commander of the Colonial Army when he fought *against* the British instead of alongside them.

In 1985, Dominion, a Richmond-based energy company, built a dam across Back Creek because the company needed water for a reservoir. Although the reservoir is closed to the public due to fluctuating water levels, the area below the reservoir

Types of Fish

Chances are you will only land rainbows here, but occasionally you will land a brown. Local anglers also report that McConaughy rainbows migrate out of Lake Moomaw into Back Creek to spawn.

Known Hatches

Back Creek supports the same hatches as most other mountain streams in the region. Anglers will find Winter Stoneflies, Blue Quills, Blue Wing Olives, Hendricksons, March Browns, Little Yellow Stoneflies, Sulfurs, Quill Gordons, Caddis, Cahills, inchworms, and terrestrials hatching throughout the year. Keep in mind that a mountain stream this large will also support a good population of baitfish like sculpins and black-nose dace as well.

Equipment to Use

Rods: 4-7 weight, 8-9 feet in length. The larger rods will help with casting streamers.
Reels: Standard mechanical, though a large fish could show you your backing given the strong current.
Lines: Weight-forward floating lines matched to the rod. Sink tips could also be used.
Leaders: 4X-6X leaders, 9 feet in length.
Wading: Although hip waders can be used in much of Back Creek, I would recommend chest waders (which can always be rolled down in the heat) and a wading stick.

Continued

Don't be misled by its name: Back Creek is as big as a river in many places. Photo by Beau Beasley.

Back Creek is a wonderful trout stream easily accessible from Route 600. Photo by Beau Beasley.

is fed cool clear water which, in essence, makes this portion of Back Creek a great tailwater fishery. Back Creek was almost totally redesigned by Dominion biologists who worked with contractors and added deep channels, improved riparian buffer zones, and generally stabilized the banks wherever possible. You'll still see some wire mesh along the shoreline, just at the water's edge, holding the banks in place. After the repairs and improvements, the VDGIF stocked the creek with fingerlings and opened the water to public fishing—even though it runs across Dominion property.

Anglers who fish Back Creek need to do so in the Special Regulation Section, which is located south of the Lower Reservoir. Other parts of Route 600 are off limits and should be avoided. The two ponds directly below the reservoir are also open to the public and have a healthy population of bass and bluegill.

When I was at Back Creek, I saw several boating anglers on these ponds and they seemed to be having a great time. Although the ponds are large, they aren't overhung with trees, so you can easily cast from shore. This assumes, of course, that for some reason you don't want to catch trout on Back Creek. After all, like Washington, anglers must choose their battles wisely.

A nice trail bordering Back Creek.
Photo by Beau Beasley.

Flies to Use

Dries: Adams #14-20, BWO #14-20, Braided Butt Damsel #10-12, Dusty's Deviant #12-16, Elk Hair Caddis #14-20, Flying Ant #10-18, Gelso's Little Black Stonefly #16-20, Lt. Cahill #14-20, Little Yellow Sally #14-20, March Brown #10-14, Murray's Mr. Rapidan #14-20, Pale Morning Dun #14-20, Quill Gordon #12-22, Stimulator #12-20, Steeves' Attract Ant #16-20, Steeves' Bark Beetle #16-20, Steeves' Crystal Butt Hopper #8-10, Steeves' Disc O' Beetle #14, Steeves' UFO #10.

Nymphs & Streamers: BH Goldilox #6-10, BH Hare's Ear #14-20, BH Prince Nymph #14-20, Bruce's Little Bow #6, Coburn's Cress Bug #14-20, Coburn's Inchworm #12-14, Dover's Peach Fly #6-10, Egg #6-20, Finn's Golden Retriever #6-10, Green Weenie #14-16, Matuka #4-10, Mickey Finn #6-10, MC2 Crayfish #4-6, Muddler Minnow #6-10, Murray's Marauder #6-10, Pheasant Tail #14-20, River Witch #6, Scud #10-18, Sculpin #4-8, Woolly Bugger #6-10.

When to Fish

Peak time is early spring through the fall. I do, however, have firsthand knowledge of anglers catching fish on dry flies during snow storms on Back Creek.

Season & Limits

There is a special regulation section on Dominion property between the two Route 600 bridges that is well over a mile long. No trout may be kept between October 1 and May 31, and anglers are restricted to using single-hook artificial lures only. From June until the end of September, general fishing rules are in effect for the entire stream.

Nearby Fly Fishing

The Jackson River is your best fishing alternative if Back Creek is too high. There is also put-and-take fishing at Blowing Springs campground.

Accommodations & Services

The largest population base near Back Creek is Warm Springs. Hot Springs, a larger town located a few miles south on Route 220, is home to Allegheny Outfitters, a full-service fly shop at the world-famous Homestead resort.

Rating

Back Creek, which owes much of its strength as a trout fishery to Dominion for its redesign of the river, rates a strong 7.

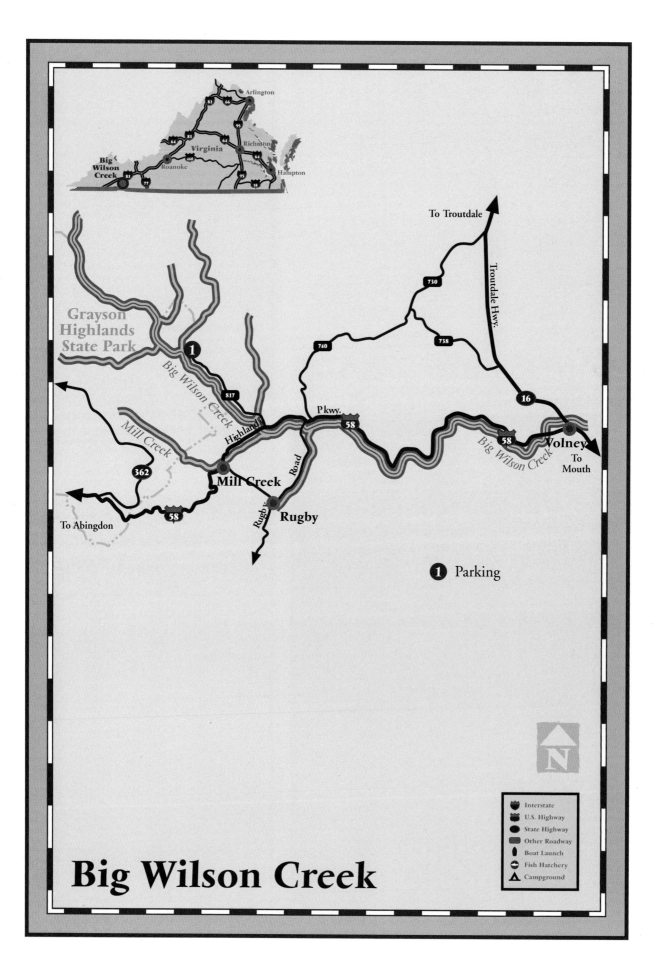

To Troutdale

730

Troutdale Hwy.

740

738

16

Pkwy.

58

58

Big Wilson Creek

Volney

To Mouth

Grayson Highlands State Park

1

Big Wilson Creek

817

Highlands

Mill Creek

362

Mill Creek

Rugby Road

58

Rugby

To Abingdon

1 Parking

Interstate
U.S. Highway
State Highway
Other Roadway
Boat Launch
Fish Hatchery
Campground

Arlington
81 66
95
Virginia
Richmond
51
66
64
Big Wilson Creek
Roanoke
81 77
Hampton
95
85

N

Big Wilson Creek

Big Wilson Creek

What makes Big Wilson Creek a mountain trout angler's dream? This stream, carrying clean, cold water in the shadow of Mount Rogers, the state's highest peak, boasts a healthy population of wild rainbow trout. Farther up Big Wilson near Grayson Highlands State Park, you'll also run into wild brook trout. But what sets Big Wilson apart is the scenery—it's simply breathtaking. Perhaps this water should be called Wilson's Big Beautiful Creek instead.

This is not novice-friendly fishing. To begin with, the tight canopy cover is a challenge. This is a mixed blessing. While the canopy makes casting a bit difficult for fly anglers, the resulting narrow stream makes spin fishing nearly impossible. Just how thick is the aforementioned canopy cover, you ask? Thick enough that I had to use my flash in the middle of a cloudless day to photograph the river. Expect that, as you pick and present the right fly, you'll place a few in the trees.

Now let us say, for argument's sake, that you've found rising fish and an area in which to cast with some degree of accuracy. Unfortunately, friend, you've only dealt with half the battle. The *real* challenge of Big Wilson is the monstrous rocks you must negotiate while fishing. My first condo had a smaller footprint than some of these massive rocks. In fact, think of fishing Big Wilson as playing a watery chess game: the huge rocks will make

Felt-soled shoes are very helpful when fishing Big Wilson Creek. Photos by Beau Beasley.

Tight cover makes casting on this trout stream a challenge.
Photo by Beau Beasley.

you back up or totally readjust your plan of attack, so the best player thinks a few moves ahead. The upside? The rocks provide for plunge pools where wary trout will run for cover.

You can reach Big Wilson Creek through Grayson Highlands State Park (where you will have to pay a fee) and hike down. Alternatively, you may take the easier way along Route 817 and hike upstream. Don't be put off by the number of houses you pass along the road on your way to the water. Although I am sure that locals fish the Big Wilson, a short time on the water will convince you that only half-crazed teenagers or slightly demented fly anglers would even attempt it.

Big Wilson Creek anglers should prepare for some rock climbing. Photo by Beau Beasley.

Types of Fish
Looking for wild rainbows and native brookies in a pristine mountain setting? You've found them.

Known Hatches
Winter Stoneflies, Blue Wing Olives, Blue Quills, Hendricksons, March Browns, Little Yellow Stoneflies, Sulfurs, Quill Gordons, Caddis, Cahills, inchworms, and terrestrials.

Equipment to Use
Rods: 2-4 weight, 7-8 feet in length.
Reels: Standard mechanical.
Lines: Weight-forward floating, matched to rod.
Leaders: 5X-7X leaders, 9 feet in length.
Wading: Hip waders are fine here.

Flies to Use
Dries: Adams #14-20, BWO #14-20, Braided Butt Damsel #10-12, Dusty's Deviant #12-16, Elk Hair Caddis #14-20, Flying Ant #10-18, Gelso's Little Black Stonefly #16-20, Lt. Cahill #14-20, Little Yellow Sally #14-20, March Brown #10-14, Murray's Mr. Rapidan #14-20, Pale Morning Dun #14-20, Quill Gordon #16-22, Stimulator #14-20, Steeves' Attract Ant #16-20, Steeves' Bark Beetle #16-20, Steeves' Crystal Butt Cricket #8-10, Steeves' Disc O' Beetle #14, Steeves' UFO #10.
Nymphs & Streamers: Beadhead Hare's Ear #14-20, Beadhead Prince Nymph #14-20, Coburn's Cress Bug #14-20, Coburn's Inchworm #12-14, Egg #8-20, Green Weenie #14-16, Mickey Finn #6-10, MC2 Crayfish #6, Muddler Minnow #8-10, Pheasant Tail #14-20, Scud #14-18, Woolly Bugger #8-10.

When to Fish
Spring and fall are always good times to fish mountain trout streams, but the summer is also a great time to hit Big Wilson. This stream has dense cover that helps to keep the water cool even during Virginia's notorious dog days.

Season & Limits
Open all year. Most of Big Wilson, at least those parts that are in Jefferson National Forest and Grayson Highlands State Park, is covered by special regulations. Only single-hook or artificial lures may be used on these portions of the creek.

Nearby Fly Fishing
Whitetop Laurel Creek and the South Fork of the Holston are your best nearby alternatives.

Accommodations & Services
Depending on where you started, you probably drove through either Marion or Damascus to get to Big Wilson Creek. The biggest population center is Abingdon, home of the top-notch Virginia Creeper Fly Shop. Other options include The Orvis Company Store and Blue Ridge Fly Fishers, both in Roanoke.

Rating
All fly anglers should give the Big Wilson a whirl. You may not catch truckloads of fish, but this water makes you rethink your entire approach to fly angling a small stream. Big Wilson rates a 7.

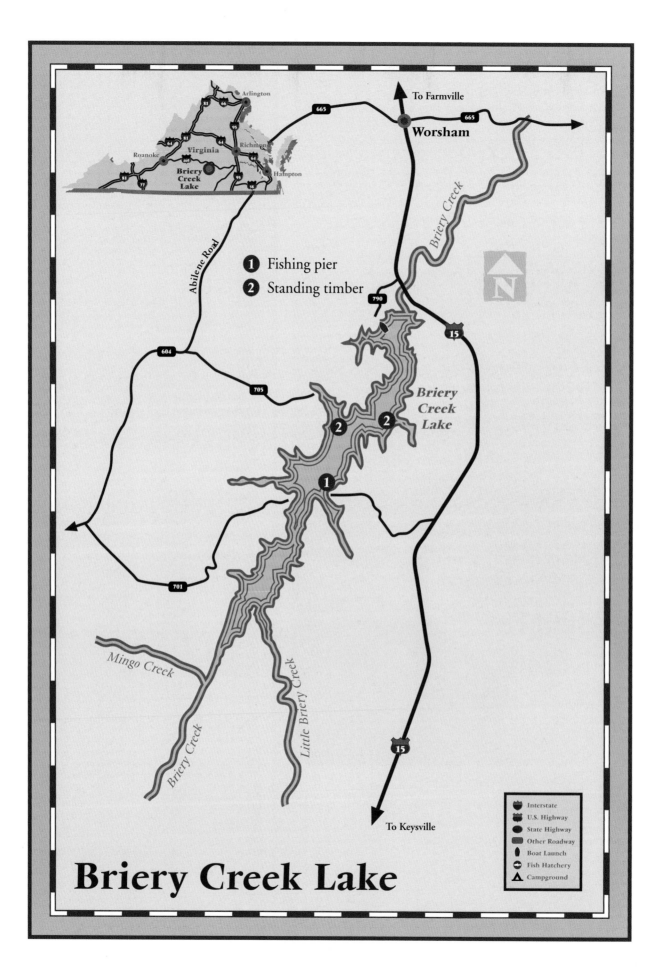

1 Fishing pier
2 Standing timber

To Farmville

665 Worsham 665

Briery Creek

790

15

Briery Creek Lake

2 2

1

15

Abilene Road

604

705

701

Mingo Creek

Briery Creek

Little Briery Creek

To Keysville

Interstate
U.S. Highway
State Highway
Other Roadway
Boat Launch
Fish Hatchery
Campground

Briery Creek Lake

Briery Creek Lake

Briery Creek Lake in Prince Edward County is an 845-acre impoundment owned by the Virginia Department of Game and Inland Fisheries and is one of the state's premier bass fisheries. The damming of Briery Creek and Little Briery Creek created Briery Creek Lake, which opened for public fishing in 1989. Much of the standing timber in this low-lying region was left in place to provide good fish habitat. Officials subsequently stocked the lake with Florida strain largemouth bass as well as crappie, red-ear sunfish, channel catfish, and chain pickerel. Was the Briery Creek Lake venture successful? Well, let's put it this way: bass in excess of 24 inches long are commonplace here.

Briery Creek Lake boasts not only good fishing but also good access for anglers with and without boats. Although boat fishing is common here, rules prohibit anything more than 10 HP trolling motors. All three fishing piers are handicap accessible. The largest pier is also covered, so anglers can have some break from the sun. Anglers will find a bathroom on site but no other facilities and no boat or canoe rentals. Looking for the perfect place to test your kayak, float tube, or canoe skills? Briery Creek Lake is the place. It's also a great place to bring kids because eager fish often hit the surface with abandon and the lack of current lessens the threat of falling out of a boat or canoe.

Crappie are great game fish.
Photo by King Montgomery.

Some of the best bass fishing in the state is on Briery Creek Lake. Photo by King Montgomery.

Anglers will see scores of standing trees on Briery Creek Lake. These trees, along with a heavy lily-pad population, provide great cover to the lake's trophy bass. Photo by Beau Beasley.

On April 7, 1865, General Robert E. Lee stayed only a stone's throw from Briery Creek in the town of Farmville as his weary Army of Northern Virginia rested. He'd recently retreated from Petersburg after the loss of the Confederate capital in Richmond, and was eagerly awaiting much-needed supplies. The supply-laden train, however, was captured by Union Cavalry General Phil Sheridan. Lee was surrounded and cut off from resupply. The following day Lee met with Union General Ulysses S. Grant at the home of one Wilbur McLean and worked out and signed preliminary surrender terms. Ironically, McLean had fled Northern Virginia with his family after Confederate General Beauregard had commandeered their home to be his headquarters during the First Battle of Manassas. McLean could fairly say, then, that the Civil War had begun in his front yard and ended in his backyard. A large historical complex at Appomattox Courthouse, where Lee surrendered, is only a 20-minute drive from Briery Creek Lake and well worth the visit.

Wilbur McLean's home, site of the signing of the Civil War armistice, is just a short drive from Briery Creek Lake at the Appomattox National Battlefield. Photo by Beau Beasley.

Types of Fish

The predominant species here is largemouth bass, though anglers will also find quite a few sunfish available as well as channel catfish and crappie.

Known Hatches

As with other warm water impoundments, everything is big: Dragonflies, other terrestrials, frogs and small baitfish.

Equipment to Use

Rods: 5-9 weight, 8 to 9½ feet in length.
Reels: Mechanical and palm.
Lines: Weight-forward floating matched to rod. Sink tips can be used here also.
Leaders: 3X-5X leaders, 9 feet in length.
Wading: Wading from the shore is not much of an option. Fish the area by boat, kayak, or even float tube.

Flies to Use

Surface water flies work well, but don't be afraid to use big streamers.
BH Goldilox #4-8, Bruce's Little Bow #2-6, Chocklett's Disc Slider #1/0, Chocklett's Gummy Minnow #6, CK Baitfish #1, Claw-Dad #2-6, Clouser Minnow #1/0-6, Cramer's Jail Bait Minnow #2-4, Finn's Golden Retriever #6-10, Hansen's Electric Frog #6, Hickey's Condor #6-12, Kreelex #2-6, MC2 Crayfish #4-6, Murray's Lead Eye Hellgrammite #6, Murray's Marauder #6, Patuxent Special #6-10, San Antonio Worm #4, Shenk's White Minnow #4-6, Super Patuxent Special #6-10, Trow's Minnow #2/0-6, Walt's Popper #2-12.

When to Fish

It can be as late as April before things start to heat up on Briery Creek Lake. By late May and into June, the top water bite is in full swing, and fish won't be put down here until late November.

Season & Limits

The lake is open all year, and anglers may keep one largemouth bass a day over 24 inches. That said, I am inclined to release everything I catch here.

Nearby Fly Fishing

Those who tire of catching warm water species can get a quick trout fix at North Creek.

Accommodations & Services

The nearby city of Farmville provides plenty of food and lodging options, but anglers will need to come prepared with all of the flies and gear they need.

Rating

Briery Creek Lake is heaven for the largemouth bass angler. I rate Briery Creek Lake a 9 on the basis of the number of trophy largemouth bass this lake produces.

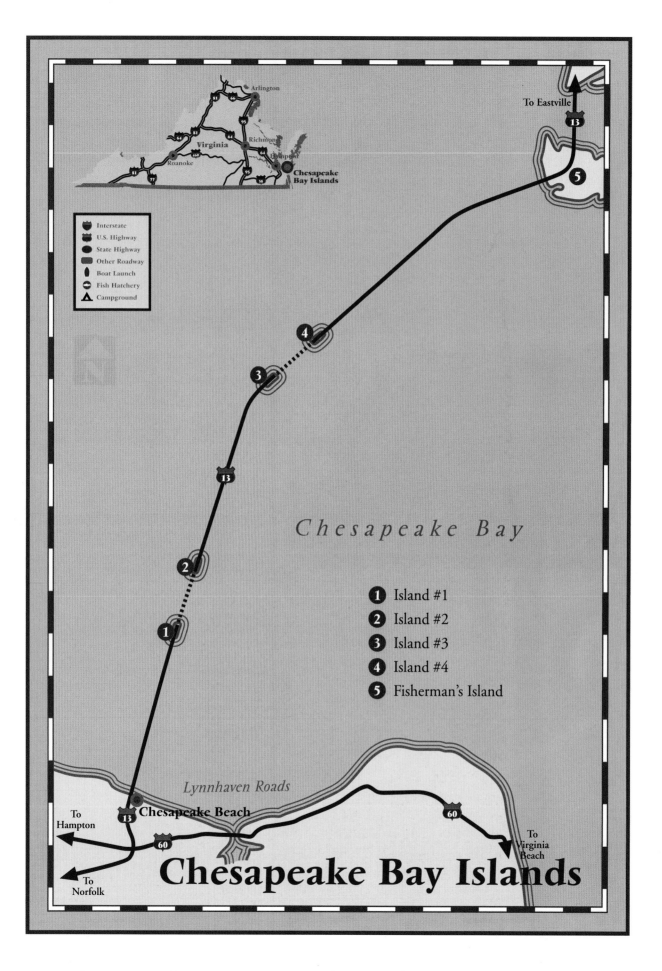

Chesapeake Bay

Lynnhaven Roads

1 Island #1
2 Island #2
3 Island #3
4 Island #4
5 Fisherman's Island

To Eastville

To Hampton

To Norfolk

Chesapeake Beach

To Virginia Beach

Legend

- Interstate
- U.S. Highway
- State Highway
- Other Roadway
- Boat Launch
- Fish Hatchery
- Campground

Arlington
Virginia
Richmond
Hampton
Roanoke
Chesapeake Bay Islands

Chesapeake Bay Islands

Chesapeake Bay Islands

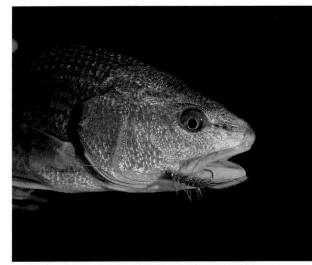

This drum fell for a B.H. Goldilox, probably thinking that it was a shrimp. Photo by Steve Probasco.

Few Virginia locales offer fly anglers the variety of saltwater fishing opportunities of the "islands" of the Chesapeake Bay Bridge Tunnel. Situated off the Virginia coast between Cape Henry and Cape Charles and extending for 20 miles, this four-land engineering marvel connects Virginia's mainland to its Eastern Shore through a series of low-level trestles and an underwater tunnel. As part of Route 13, these two sections of tunnel offer Virginia drivers the chance to travel nearly 100 feet below sea level—though I for one would rather not think about that while actually doing so. In fact, I find myself watching the walls as I am driving along just to make sure that they're not leaking. I'm not sure what I would do if I actually did spot a leak—it's not as if I could back out!

The "islands," as they are commonly known, are a number of enormous manmade rock piles built to support the Chesapeake Bay Bridge Tunnel as it enters and exits the water. Each of the islands covers about five acres and serves as outstanding habitat for all manner of sea life. I have fished these islands several times with saltwater fly fishing guide Captain Tommy Mattioli, and I can tell you that they are well worth the trip.

Captain Tommy Mattioli with a striper caught near one of the four "islands" that support the Chesapeake Bay Bridge Tunnel. Photo by Beau Beasley.

John Johnson, the author's father-in-law, with his first striper caught on a fly. Photo by Beau Beasley.

Schoolie stripers can be caught year-round off the "islands." Photo by Steve Probasco.

Anglers can choose their island fishing approach. One method consists of anchoring up to a likely looking point and casting sinking or intermediate lines into a moving tide to search for feeding fish. Another method is to drift alongside an island with the current and cast flies into the surf as it recedes from the rocky island shore. Often large fish lie just a few feet off the islands in the hopes of ambushing baitfish that stray too far from the safety of the rocks. Finally, fly anglers can observe the bird life and look for stripers, blues, and other fish that literally chase baitfish right out of the water. Anglers may find casting surface flies and streamers both exciting and frustrating as fish often bite through the line or miss the fly altogether in the mad feeding frenzy.

Baitfish patterns like the one seen here mimic bunker fish and are very effective on the Chesapeake Bay. Photo by Melissa Newsome.

Types of Fish
Stripers, bluefish, cobia, gray seatrout, speckled trout, flounder, croaker, drum, spade fish, false albacore.

Known Baitfish
Atlantic menhaden (bunker) and other small baitfish.

Equipment to Use
Rods: 8-10 weight rods, 9-10 feet in length.
Reels: Mechanical and large arbor reels.
Lines: Fast to intermediate sink tips matched to rod, as well as sinking lines of 200-400 grains.
Leaders: 10- to 30-lb. test leaders 3-5 feet in length (wire leaders should be used if fishing for blues).
Wading: You'll need a boat as wading is not possible.

Flies to Use
Bruce's Bay Anchovie #2, Bruce's Crystal Shrimp #1/0, Clouser Minnow #2/0-4, DuBiel's Finesse Fly #2-4, DuBiel's Lil'hadden #1/0-2, DuBiel's Red-Ducer #1/0-2, Lefty's Deceiver #3/0-2, Lefty's Half and Half, #3/0-2, Russell's Mussel #1/0-1, Tommy's Crease Fly #2/0-2, Tommy's Eel Fly #2/0-1/0, Trow's Minnow Saltwater #3/0-6.

When to Fish
Fishing on the Chesapeake Bay offers so many opportunities that it's hard to know when to go. Ultimately it's a question of what you are fishing for. Many anglers pursue stripers here, which have good runs in the spring and fall. October through mid-December is prime time for big stripers. Keep in mind that you can catch nearly everything in the Bay.

Season & Limits
Open all year. Limits and sizes will depend on species and the time of year that you're fishing.

Nearby Fly Fishing
If the weather is a little rough in the Bay, you can always opt for Rudee Inlet or the Lynnhaven River. Both are great alternatives when you need a saltwater fix and the wind isn't cooperating.

Accommodations & Services
There are abundant services as well as fly shops and guides in nearby Virginia Beach, Newport News, and Hampton.

Rating
The Chesapeake Bay Islands can run hot and cold. During the dog days of summer, fly fishing can be long and tiresome, but during the spring and fall when the striper migrations occur, these islands rate a 10.

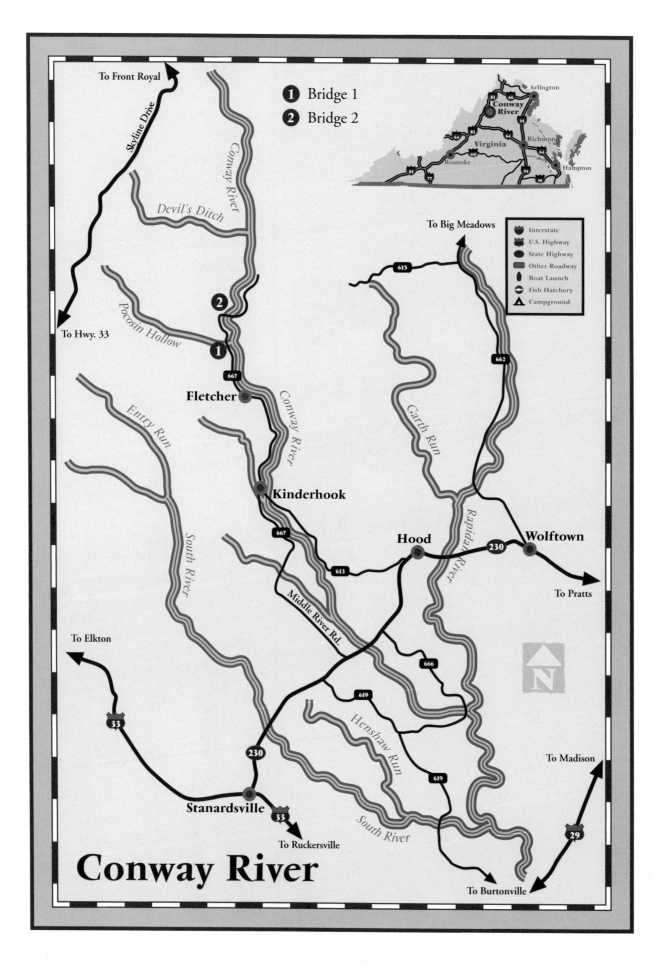

Conway River

Conway River
(or Middle River)

The Conway River, known as Middle River by locals, flows through both the Rapidan Wildlife Management Area as well as the Shenandoah National Park. It's the sort of water that brookie anglers love to fish—but don't be too surprised if you pull out the occasional brown. Perhaps more aptly called a creek, the Conway has steep grades and large rocks that eager anglers will need to negotiate carefully. The water here is often low and almost always clear, giving the local brook trout every advantage. You'll find pools alongside the rock-hewn banks, where the trout lie in wait for a meal to float by. While fishing the Conway, I found myself wishing for more structure in addition to the rocks, because these often cause the rushing water to boil or turn in a haphazard direction making effective drifts quite difficult. When I did find the occasional tree lying in the river, it seemed that the wily trout in the lie knew just how to hide beneath the branches in such a way that by the time he rushed to take my fly, I had to move my offering before it was grabbed by the aforementioned branch. (Or perhaps I'm just a lousy angler. No, that couldn't be it. Those must have been exceptionally bright trout.)

King Montgomery with a trout caught near Shenandoah National Park. Photo courtesy King Montgomery.

The Conway is a popular trout stream in Shenandoah National Park. Photo by King Montgomery.

Crayfish are in both warm and cold water streams throughout Virginia. Photo by Beau Beasley.

If the Conway has one drawback, it's a lack of parking. Route 667 runs adjacent to a number of private homes (some of which can only be accessed by swinging bridges that traverse the river), so be careful where you fish. Private property is labeled fairly well—too well, I thought with envy as I spied a rope swing tied to an overhanging tree dangling over a large pool that appeared to be home to a number of fat, finning trout.

The easiest parking area is near Pocosin Hollow just past the first bridge. The trail leading to Pocosin Hollow is popular with hikers, so just because you see a few cars parked here doesn't mean you'll have a crowded day on the river. The next best place to park is near the second bridge, which has easy pull-outs and shoulders to park on. From this bridge it's a short (¾ of a mile) hike to the end of the road. Drive to the end of Route 667 to get the lay of the land. You may be able to find a closer place to park by doing so, and be sure to check for no parking signs first.

The upside to all this added hiking is that the Conway has fewer visitors than its famous cousin, the Rapidan River. Yes, the Conway River is less well known than some nearby streams. No, the trout don't seem to mind—and neither should you.

Hiring a guide is a wise choice on your first fishing trip in the Shenandoah National Park. Photo by King Montgomery.

Types of Fish
You'll find rainbow trout here along with the occasional brown. The Conway used to be brook trout water, so you might catch a brookie every now and then. Unfortunately, however, the brookies just don't do as well in warmer water as the stocked rainbows.

Known Hatches
No big surprises: the hatch on the Conway is consistent with other mountain streams in the Shenandoah National Park. Look for Winter Stoneflies, Blue Quills, Hendricksons, March Browns, Little Yellow Stoneflies, Sulfurs, Quill Gordons, Caddis, Cahills, inchworms, and terrestrials.

Equipment to Use
Rods: 3-4 weight, 7½-8 feet in length.
Reels: Standard mechanical.
Lines: Weight-forward floating, matched to rod.
Leaders: 5X-7X leaders, 9 feet in length.
Wading: Hip waders are fine here.

Flies to Use
Dries: Adams #14-20, BWO #14-20, Dusty's Deviant #12-16, Elk Hair Caddis #14-20, Flying Ant #10-18, Gelso's Little Black Stonefly #16-20, Lt. Cahill #14-20, Little Yellow Sally #14-20, March Brown #10-14, Murray's Mr. Rapidan #14-20, Pale Morning Dun #14-20, Quill Gordon #12-22, Stimulator #14-20, Steeves' Attract Ant #16-20, Steeves' Bark Beetle #16-20, Steeves' Crystal Butt Hopper #8-10.
Nymphs & Streamers: BH Goldilox #8-10, BH Hare's Ear #14-20, BH Prince Nymph #14-20, Coburn's Cress Bug #14-20, Coburn's Inchworm #12-14, Egg #6-20, Green Weenie #14-16, Mickey Finn #6-10, Muddler Minnow #8-10, Pheasant Tail #14-20, Scud #10-18, Sculpin #6-8, Woolly Bugger #6-10.

When to Fish
The Conway should start fishing well by the end of March and go straight through November. Be aware, however, that the water can be very low from July through the beginning of September.

Season & Limits
As in the rest of the Shenandoah National Park, no trout under nine inches may be kept at any time, and you may never keep more than six. Do yourself and everyone else a favor: get your fish at the grocery store, and leave these fish in the river.

Nearby Fly Fishing
Alternatives abound throughout the Shenandoah National Park. Other nearby streams include the Rose, the Rapidan, the Hughes, the Hazel, and the Robinson.

Accommodations & Services
Sperryville is the closest town, but you'll need to get your flies and fishing information from Rhodes Fly Shop in Warrenton or The Castaway Company in Culpeper.

Rating
The Conway is a good little river that you should at least fish once. It's close to the Appalachian Trail, so you can always get in a good hike if the fish aren't biting. The Conway rates a 6.

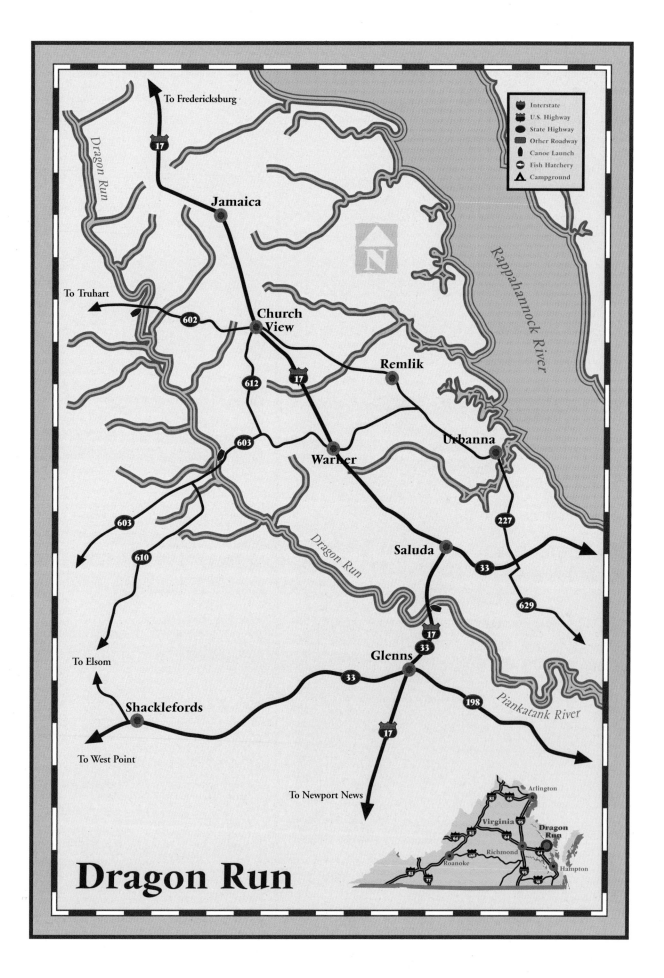

Dragon Run

Dragon Run

Dragon Run is a difficult place to describe to those who have never seen it. "The Dragon," as it is known by locals, may seem at first blush to be an uninviting watershed. In fact, local plantation owners used to discourage their slaves from attempting to run away by spreading the tale that dragons lived in the local river. Who would believe that, you ask? Let me tell you that an afternoon spent floating through this unique fishery would be enough to convince anyone that there just might be monsters lurking here.

Dragon Run is the headwaters of the Piankatank River and runs serpentine ever so slowly through the counties of King and Queen, Essex, Gloucester, and Middlesex. Underground springs and runoff from the surrounding swampland are at least partially responsible for feeding the area. As a result of careful land management by local landowners, the area has remained virtually unchanged since before the country was founded. Large cypress trees and dark tannic water, along with a shoreline almost totally covered with marsh grass or thick brush, make Dragon Run appear spooky and almost impenetrable.

Though I didn't see a single "no fishing" sign on the river, plenty of "no hunting" popped up along the way—an indication that private land does indeed back up to the area despite the wild and untamed scenery. Don't be surprised to find the occasional tree stand—complete with ladder—built into one of the sturdy cypress trees.

Dragon Run is a warm water angler's paradise. Healthy largemouth bass and bluegill as large as your hand call this area home, as well as voracious gar. But remember that tidal fluctuations make the Dragon inaccessible in a standard boat with an outboard motor, except at high tide. Even then, the uninformed could find themselves hitting a cypress tree stump just below the water's surface. The best way to fish the Dragon Run area effectively is by canoe, kayak, or johnboat.

Captain Chris Newsome with a largemouth bass.
Photo by Beau Beasley.

Dragon Run's quiet waters lead into the Piankatank River and eventually Chesapeake Bay. Photo by Beau Beasley.

Types of Fish
Largemouth bass, bluegill, bowfin, longnose gar, perch, chain pickerel.

Known Hatches
There is very little information available about the Dragon Run fishery apart from a few conservation websites. It is safe, however, to assume that most of your warm water insects will appear here as well as various baitfish.

Equipment to Use
Rods: 6-8 weight, 9 feet in length.
Reels: Standard disc drag.
Lines: Floating to match rod weight.
Leaders: 1X-3X leaders, 9 feet in length.
Wading: Not recommended.

Flies to Use
BH Goldilox #4-8, Bruce's Little Bow #2-6, Claw-Dad #2-6, Chocklett's Disc Slider #1/0, Chocklett's Gummy Minnow #6, CK Baitfish #1, Clouser Minnow #1/0-6, Cramer's Jail Bait Minnow #2-4, Finn's Golden Retriever #6-10, Hansen's Electric Frog #6, Hickey's Condor #6-12, Kreelex #2-6, MC2 Crayfish #4-6, Murray's Lead Eye Hellgrammite #6, Murray's Marauder #6, Patuxent Special #6-10, San Antonio Worm #4, Shenk's White Minnow #4-6, Super Patuxent Special #6-10, Trow's Minnow, Walt's Popper #2-12.

When to Fish
Dragon Run can be fished year-round, though April through November seem to be the best months.

Seasons & Limits
Open all year, check local game laws.

Nearby Fly Fishing
The easiest place to fish nearby is the Piankatank River, which is fed by Dragon Run. The lower portion of the Chesapeake Bay near Gwynn Island is also available.

Accommodations & Services
The best place for basic necessities is the small town of Saluda.

Rating
Having fished all over Virginia, I can say without hesitation that I have never seen anything like Dragon Run in the Old Dominion. With its variety of fish and unique scenery, Dragon Run easily rates an 8.

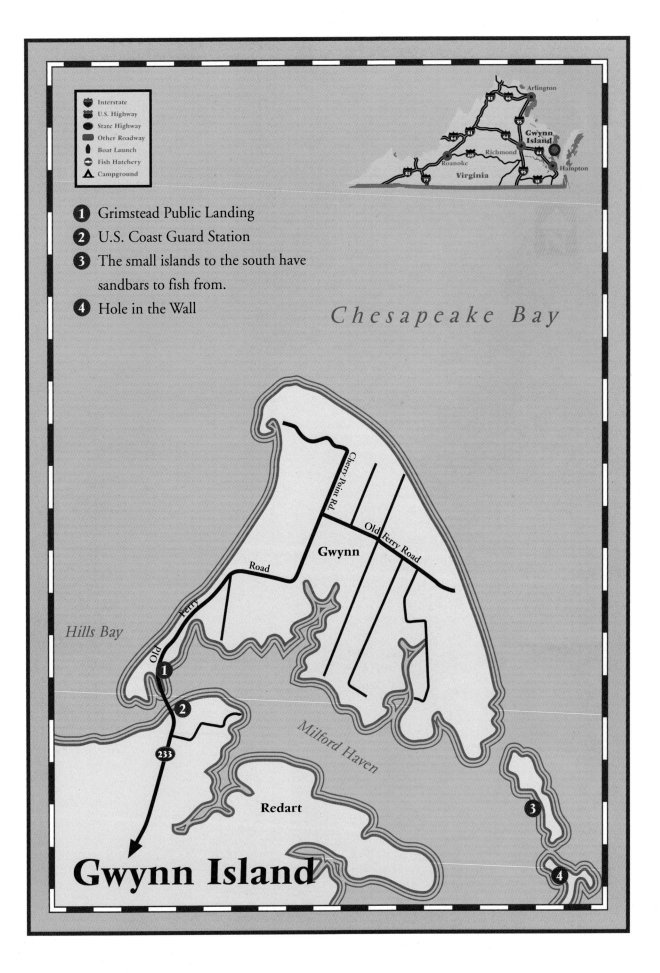

Interstate
U.S. Highway
State Highway
Other Roadway
Boat Launch
Fish Hatchery
Campground

1 Grimstead Public Landing
2 U.S. Coast Guard Station
3 The small islands to the south have sandbars to fish from.
4 Hole in the Wall

Chesapeake Bay

Cherry Point Rd.

Old Ferry Road

Gwynn

Road

Ferry

Old

Hills Bay

1

2

233

Milford Haven

Redart

3

4

Gwynn Island

Gwynn Island

Chesapeake Bay anglers have so much water to choose from that many places go untouched and unnoticed by most. Gwynn Island is just such a place. Connected to the rest of Mathews County by the Gwynn Island Bridge, Gwynn Island is a unique fishery. With Milford Haven to the south, Hills Bay to the west, and the Chesapeake Bay surrounding the island on its northern and eastern boundaries, anglers will find good fishing in every direction.

Though it's impossible to determine exactly where the Chesapeake Bay ends and the Piankatank River begins, Gwynn Island lies at the mouth of the Piankatank River and directly across from Stingray Point in nearby Middlesex County. Fly anglers unfamiliar with the island can simply cast to any of the surrounding structure they see once they find a likely-looking spot. Plenty of old docks and defunct piers exist to choose from. It was near one of these old piers that I landed my first flounder on the fly. Anglers can also hop out of their boats or kayaks and wade on many of the nearby sandbars.

Gwynn Island may be new to many Mid-Atlantic anglers, but trust me: the island has a history. Not long after Captain John Smith arrived in the region from England, he was badly injured by a stingray near what is now known as—can you guess?—Stingray Point directly across from Gwynn Island.

Captain Chris Newsome with a flounder caught near Gwynn Island. Photo by Melissa Newsome.

Look for changes—bends, structure—in the shoreline, and you'll usually find the fish. Photo by Beau Beasley.

Captain Tony Harding with a nice striper caught near Gwynn Island. Photo by Beau Beasley.

Old piers often hold fish. Photo by Beau Beasley.

Smith ran the stingray through with his sword, but not until after he had received a nasty wound. His party, fearing he would die, chose to bury their good captain on Gwynn Island. In fact Smith did not die then. Between 1607 and 1609, he and his crew explored and mapped the entire Chesapeake Bay—an extraordinary feat when we consider that they mapped over 3,000 miles and visited dozens of Native American communities from an open boat. Smith declared that "heaven and earth never agreed better to frame a more perfect place for man's habitation." Anglers who discover the unique Gwynn Island fishery might be inclined to agree with him.

Seagulls can often mark feeding fish, although this one seems to be taking a break. Photo by Beau Beasley.

Types of Fish
Stripers, blues, gray seatrout, speckled trout, flounder, croaker, and puppy drum.

Known Baitfish
Anglers fishing in and around Gwynn Island can expect to see menhaden, shrimp, squid, crabs, a variety of small baitfish, and eels.

Equipment to Use
Rods: 6-9 weight, 9 to 9½ feet in length.
Reels: Standard disc drag; large arbor works better with larger species.
Lines: Fast-intermediate sinking lines matched to rod. A 200-grain sinking line will work in some places.
Leaders: 1X-3X, 9 feet in length.
Wading: Wading in and around Gwynn Island is generally done in conjunction with a boat or a kayak. Wet wading is common in this case, however full chest waders are an option. Wading off oyster bars and near old pilings, as well as on one of the many surrounding sandbars, is also a good idea.

Flies to Use
Bruce's Bay Anchovie #2, Bruce's Crystal Shrimp #1/0, Clouser Minnow #2/0-4, DuBiel's Finesse Fly #2-4, DuBiel's Lil'hadden #1/0-2, DuBiel's Red-Ducer #1/0-2, Lefty's Deceiver #2/0-2, Lefty's Half and Half #2/0-2, Russell's Mussel #1/0-1, Tommy's Crease Fly #2/0-2, Tommy's Eel Fly #2/0-1/0, Trow's Minnow Saltwater #2/0-6.

When to Fish
Gwynn Island can be fished at any time. Prime times are late spring and throughout the fall. Bluebird winter days can also produce fish.

Season & Limits
Open all year. Size limits will be determined by the particular species you are targeting.

Nearby Fly Fishing
Just around the corner from Gwynn Island is the mouth of the Piankatank River. If you have access to a boat, you should be able to fish both pieces of water.

Accommodations & Services
Though limited food and lodging exists on Gwynn Island proper, Mathews County boasts several quaint lodging and dining options (check out www.visitmathews.com). Fly anglers will find limited gear available near Gwynn Island. Queens Creek Outfitters in nearby Cobbs Creek is the place to find flies or fly lines.

Rating
I rate Gwynn Island a 7. With the right weather it could hit an 8 for those willing to give this great fishery a try.

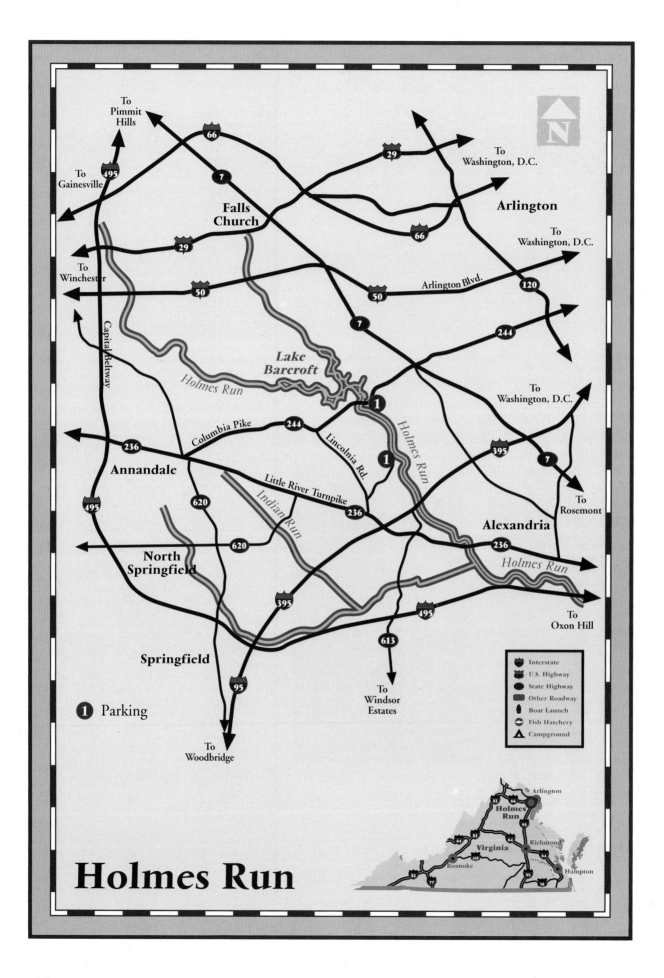

Holmes Run

Holmes Run

Holmes Run is a quiet little creek that runs from the dam at Lake Barcroft in Fairfax County, directly off of Columbia Pike and smack-dab in the heart of Northern Virginia. Far from where you would expect to land a handsome trout, this stream is one of the most picturesque in Virginia—sitting in the middle of suburbia, hiding right out in the open. Holmes Run starts just below Lake Barcroft in its upper section and extends nearly 1½ miles before it crosses into Cameron Run in Alexandria.

Like most waters, Holmes Run has its share of problems. In my opinion, however, its ups outweigh its downs. What works: the stream is easy to access, it has good cover for the fish, and its waters allow for easy wading. I found Holmes Run surprisingly deep in some places—up to my waist, as a matter of fact. And there are several pools in varying widths and depths to choose from. There are also classic runs and riffles and a smattering of large boulders for wary trout to hide behind. The biggest surprise, though, is the serene beauty of this place. In some parts it has tall gorge-like sides and a vast array of rock exposures.

Types of Fish
Holmes Run is stocked with rainbow trout at least twice a year by the VDGIF.

Known Hatches
Blue Wing Olives, Blue Quills, March Browns, Sulfurs, Quill Gordons, Caddis, Cahills, and terrestrials. Remember, though, that these are hatchery fish and therefore may not pay as much attention to hatches as wild trout might.

Equipment to Use
Rods: 2-4 weight, 7½-8 feet in length.
Reels: Standard mechanical.
Lines: Weight-forward floating, matched to rod. You may use split shot in a few places in early spring, though you do not need a sink-tip line.
Leaders: 4X-5X leaders, 9 feet in length.
Wading: Hip waders are fine here.
Continued

A long pool on Holmes Run offers plenty of room for the local trout. Photo by Beau Beasley.

Urban serenity, only ten minutes from Northern Virginia's Capital Beltway. Photo by Beau Beasley.

Large trees line the banks, and ferns and small undergrowth help protect the banks from being worn down. If not for the occasional high rise condominium that intermittently breaks through the upper treeline, you'd think you were 200 miles outside the nation's capital instead of just 20.

Unfortunately Holmes Run contains no native trout. The warmer-than-ideal water that flows from the top of the Lake Barcroft Dam does not allow for naturally occurring fish populations, so all the fish here are hatchery trout. In fact, you can thank the Northern Virginia Chapter of Trout Unlimited, the Fairfax County Park Authority, and the Virginia Department of Game and Inland Fisheries (VDGIF) that Holmes Run contains any trout at all. The Northern Virginia TU chapter took on work at this creek in January 2003 when the VDGIF decided to make it a delayed-harvest stream.

Coming from Columbia Pike in Annandale, watch for the sharp right-hand turn to enter Holmes Run. If you pass Fairfax County Fire Station 10 on the right, you have gone too far. To enter Holmes Run from the lower end in Alexandria, turn left on North Chambliss Street from Lincolnia Road and park at the end of the road. There is a trail that runs parallel to the stream that provides easy access.

This trout fell to a Woolly Bugger. Photo by Beau Beasley.

Flies to Use

Dries: Adams #14-20, BWO #14-20, Braided Butt Damsel #10-12, Dusty's Deviant #12-16, Elk Hair Caddis #14-20, Flying Ant #10-18, Gelso's Little Black Stonefly #16-20, Lt. Cahill #14-20, Little Yellow Sally #14-20, March Brown #10-14, Murray's Mr. Rapidan #14-20, Pale Morning Dun #14-20, Quill Gordon #12-22, Stimulator #12-20, Steeves' Attract Ant #16-20, Steeves' Bark Beetle #16-20, Steeves' Crystal Butt Hopper #8-10, Steeves' Disc O' Beetle #14, Steeves' UFO #10.

Nymphs & Streamers: BH Goldilox #6-10, BH Hare's Ear #14-20, BH Prince Nymph #14-20, Bruce's Little Bow #6, Coburn's Cress Bug #14-20, Coburn's Inchworm #12-14, Egg #6-20, Finn's Golden Retriever #6-10, Green Weenie #14-16, Matuka #4-10, Mickey Finn #6-10, MC2 Crayfish #4-6, Muddler Minnow #6-10, Murray's Marauder #6-10, Pheasant Tail #14-20, River Witch #6, Scud #10-18, Sculpin #4-8, Woolly Bugger #6-10.

When to Fish

You can fish Holmes Run year-round, but it can get quite low in the summer. This water tends to run a bit warm because it is fed from the top of Lake Barcroft rather than the bottom.

Season & Limits

Holmes Run is entirely delayed harvest and only single-hook artificial lures may be used. No fish may be kept between October 1 and May 31. You do need a trout stamp to fish this stream. You don't need to feel guilty about taking a few fish home when it's legal. The water here can get quite warm, so it is doubtful that many of the trout would make it through a hard summer.

Nearby Fly Fishing

The closest fishing spot to Holmes Run is Accotink Creek, just off Braddock Road on the other side of Interstate 495 (the Beltway). For those willing to drive about 90 minutes, you can also fish in the Shenandoah National Park or the Rappahannock in Fredericksburg.

Accommodations & Services

Nearby Annandale and Alexandria are home to more hotels and restaurants than you could possibly ever need. The closest fly shops are Orvis Tysons Corner and LL Bean at Tysons Corner Center. Orvis Clarendon and The Angler's Lie are in Arlington. You'll find The Trophy Room, a relatively new fly shop, in the heart of historic Old Town Alexandria.

Rating

Holmes Run rates a 6, but its location makes it well worth the trip for those who need a quick trout fix.

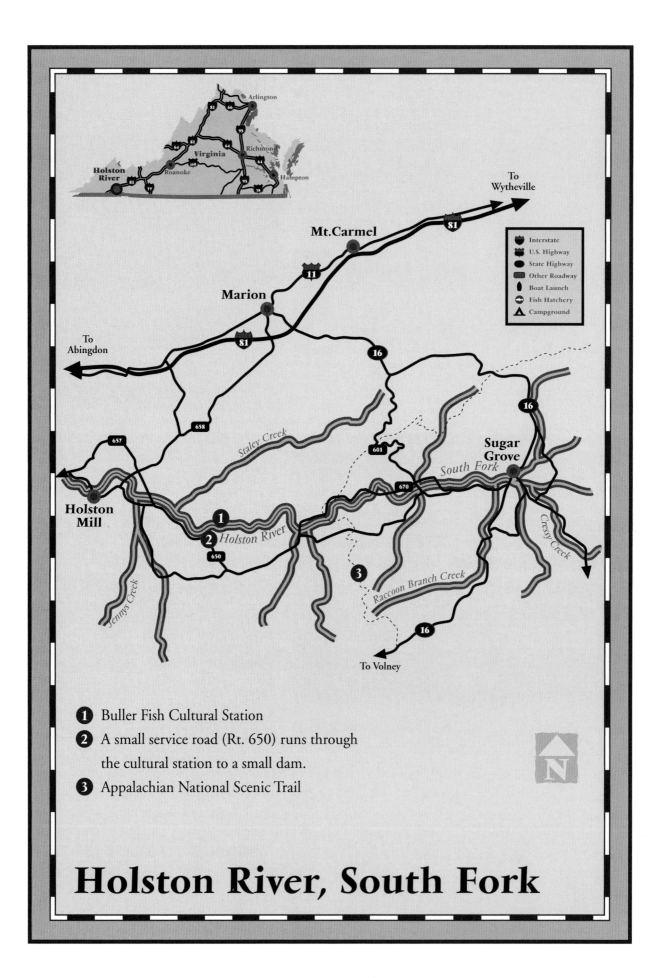

To Wytheville

Mt.Carmel

Marion

To Abingdon

Sugar Grove

South Fork

Holston Mill

Staley Creek

Holston River

Jennys Creek

Raccoon Branch Creek

Cressy Creek

To Volney

1 Buller Fish Cultural Station

2 A small service road (Rt. 650) runs through the cultural station to a small dam.

3 Appalachian National Scenic Trail

Interstate
U.S. Highway
State Highway
Other Roadway
Boat Launch
Fish Hatchery
Campground

N

Holston River, South Fork

Holston River
South Fork

T he Holston River has three forks—North, Middle, and South—but I've chosen to concentrate on the South Fork of the Holston because it is the best-known Virginia trout water of the three. The North and the Middle forks both boast good populations of smallmouth bass, but access to these forks is limited because most of the river is surrounded by private land. By contrast, the South Fork of the Holston is much colder than her sisters because it's fed primarily by huge limestone springs flowing from nearby Sugar Grove. And it has very good cover, which also helps to keep the water cool all year, even in the heat of summer. Although it's true that great trout fishing exists on the South Fork of the Holston in Tennessee as well, that will have to wait for another book.

Anglers will find two different special regulation trout fishing sections within the upper portions of the river. In the largest section, anglers may use only single-hook artificial lures, and there is a creel limit of two fish per day and a size limit of at least 16 inches. This section is approximately four miles long, extending from 500 feet above the dam at the Buller Fish Cultural Station upstream to the upper Jefferson National Forest boundary (above the crossing of the Appalachian Trail). Both rainbow and brown trout are available in this section of the South Fork.

The second section of special regulation trout fishing is for catch-and-release only (and again, anglers may use only single-hook artificial lures). This section of the South Fork lies within the boundaries of the Virginia Department of Game and Inland Fisheries' Buller Fish Cultural Station. It extends from the concrete dam downstream to the lower boundary of the Cultural Station. This area provides excellent trophy trout for all anglers and provides year-round trout fishing with easy access through the Buller property. If you absolutely have to take a few fish home, you'll find a put-and-take section that extends above the dam for about 500 feet. Confused? Look for signs posted streamside on the trees, or ask for guidance from one of the helpful folks at the Buller Fish Cultural Station, which is in sight of the river.

The South Fork of the Holston River is home to some of the state's best trout fishing. Photo by King Montgomery.

Types of Fish
This fishery is known for good rainbows as well as healthy brown trout, some of which can be quite large. You can also catch smallies.

Known Hatches
Winter Stoneflies, Blue Wing Olives, Blue Quills, Hendricksons, March Browns, Little Yellow Stoneflies, Sulfurs, Quill Gordons, Caddis, Cahills, inchworms, terrestrials, and Green Drakes.

Equipment to Use
Rods: 4-7 weight, 7½-9 feet in length.
Reels: Standard mechanical.
Lines: Weight-forward floating, matched to rod.
Leaders: 4X-7X leaders, 9 feet in length.
Wading: Chest waders are the way to go when fishing the Holston.

Flies to Use
Dries: Adams #14-20, BWO #14-20, Braided Butt Damsel #10-12, Dusty's Deviant #12-16, Elk Hair Caddis #14-20, Flying Ant #10-18, Gelso's Little Black Stonefly #16-20, Lt. Cahill #14-20, Little Yellow Sally #14-20, March Brown #10-14, Murray's Mr. Rapidan #14-20, Pale Morning Dun #14-20, Quill Gordon #12-22, Stimulator #12-20, Steeves' Attract Ant #16-20, Steeves' Bark Beetle #16-20, Steeves' Crystal Butt Hopper #8-10, Steeves' Disc O' Beetle #14, Steeves' UFO #10.
Nymphs & Streamers: BH Goldilox #6-10, BH Hare's Ear #14-20, BH Prince Nymph #14-20, Bruce's Little Bow #6, Coburn's Cress Bug #14-20, Coburn's Inchworm #12-14, Egg #6-20, Finn's Golden Retriever #6-10, Green Weenie #14-16, Matuka #4-10, Mickey Finn #6-10, MC2 Crayfish #4-6, Muddler Minnow #6-10, Murray's Marauder #6-10, Pheasant Tail #14-20, River Witch #6, Scud #10-18, Sculpin #4-8, Woolly Bugger #6-10.

When to Fish
Fishing is best in early spring, but don't overlook this top-notch fishery in summer. As with most trout streams, the summer heat can put a strain on the river. But by the fall the Holston is back in full swing sometimes well into November.

Season & Limits
Different rules apply depending on what section of the river you're fishing. The VDGIF is diligent about posting its special trout water so look on stream bank trees for postings. If you're unsure of game laws when fishing, always be conservative and release your fish as soon as you can.

Nearby Fly Fishing
Alternatives include Whitetop Laurel and Big Wilson Creek. The Holston also has excellent water in Tennessee.

Accommodations & Services
The closest place for food and fuel is the town of Marion. The closest fly shops are The Orvis Company Store and Blue Ridge Fly Fishers, both in Roanoke. You will also find all the flies and advice you need at The Virginia Creeper Fly Shop in Abingdon.

Rating
The South Fork of the Holston ranks an easy 9.

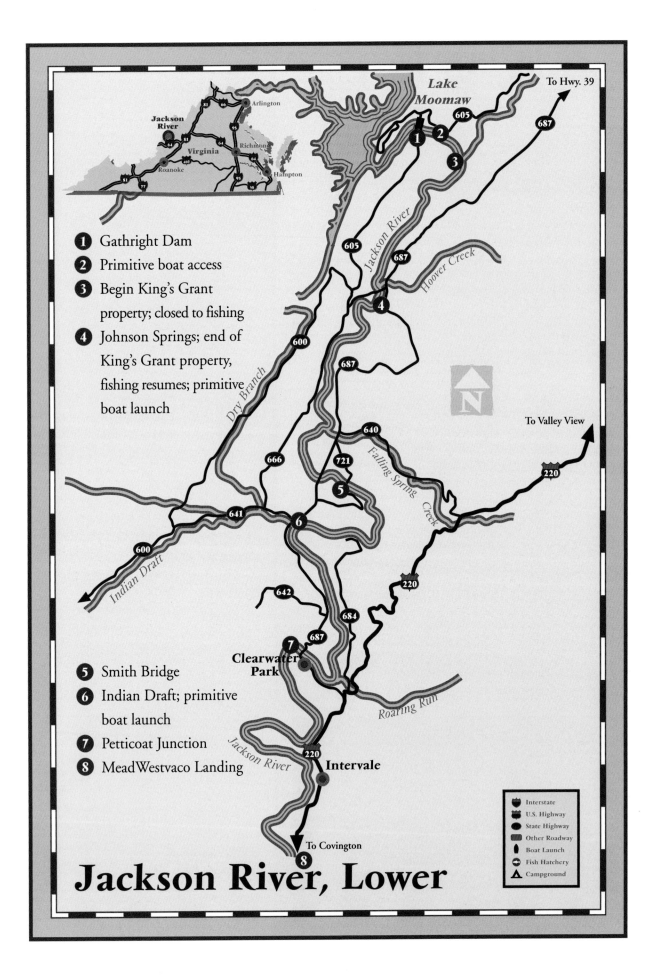

To Hwy. 39

Lake Moomaw

1 Gathright Dam

2 Primitive boat access

3 Begin King's Grant property; closed to fishing

4 Johnson Springs; end of King's Grant property, fishing resumes; primitive boat launch

605

Jackson River

687

Hoover Creek

605

600

Dry Branch

687

To Valley View

640

666

721

220

641

600

Indian Draft

6

642

684

220

Falling Spring Creek

5 Smith Bridge

6 Indian Draft; primitive boat launch

7 Petticoat Junction

8 MeadWestvaco Landing

687

Clearwater Park

Roaring Run

Jackson River

220

Intervale

To Covington

8

	Interstate
	U.S. Highway
	State Highway
	Other Roadway
	Boat Launch
	Fish Hatchery
	Campground

Jackson River, Lower

Jackson River

Virginia

Arlington

Richmond

Roanoke

Hampton

Jackson River
Lower Section

The lower portion of the Jackson River is a tailrace that begins at the base of Gathright Dam. The dam normally releases 58-degree water from Lake Moomaw via a 200-foot tower. Released directly below the dam, this water has two very positive effects: First, the river receives 58-degree water year-round, which the trout love. Second, because controlled releases carefully regulate the influx, this part of the Jackson can be perfectly suitable for fishing when other waters within 100 miles are out of their banks after heavy rains. Anglers will need written permission from the Army Corps of Engineers' Gathright Dam office to fish directly below the dam. The fishing permit is free and is good for a year. Too busy to pick up a permit? Don't chance it. Local sheriff's deputies patrol this area daily.

The area of the Jackson directly below the dam has bathrooms and a place to launch small boats, but that's where the good news ends. In 1996, local landowners filed a claim contending that they not only owned the river bottom but the fish in the river as well, and that this ownership was passed on to new owners as they purchased the property. Before this issue arose, guides and other anglers would float the river and fish as they went along. Much to everyone's surprise, the case

A view of the lower Jackson River as seen from the Gathright Dam. Photo by Beau Beasley.

Anglers will find plenty of room to cast on the Jackson. Photo by Beau Beasley.

If you fish the Jackson in the middle of the week, you might find yourself alone on the river. Photo by Beau Beasley.

went all the way to the Virginia Supreme Court, which issued a landmark decision commonly referred to as the King's Grant or King's Crown decision. The Court stated that not only did local landowners possess the bottom of the river (effectively preventing anglers from anchoring their boats), but the fish in the river were also their property. These sections are well marked along the river—and I must say that they are the most ominous signs I've ever seen as an angler. If you see one of these warnings, you would do well to heed it.

The King's Grant area begins roughly ¾ of a mile below the dam and continues to Johnson Springs where it officially ends. Anglers can fish from here to the MeadWestvaco Landing near Covington. There is a chance you will be approached by landowners who claim King's Grant rights below Johnson Springs, however these folks were not part of the lawsuit and their claims were not validated by the court. Having said that, if you are approached by a landowner, be polite and move on regardless of where you are on the river.

Anglers will find easy access available to several other sections of the lower Jackson, including Johnson Springs, Jack's Island, Smith Bridge, Indian Draft, and Petticoat Junction. Should you choose to fish directly below the Gathright Dam, you ought to call ahead to learn what flows they are releasing. Flows above 400 cfs, although rare, mean that the area directly below the dam is too swift to fish safely. For the latest information on scheduled releases (updated daily by 9 a.m.), call 540-965-4117.

Tom Brown of the Virginia Council of Trout Unlimited hooked up on the lower Jackson. Photo by Beau Beasley.

Types of Fish
You'll find mostly healthy rainbows here, but you can also catch some nice browns. Every once in a great while you may even find a brookie.

Known Hatches
Blue Quills, Hendricksons, March Browns, Little Yellow Stoneflies, Sulfurs, Quill Gordons, Caddis, Cahills, inchworms, and terrestrials are major food components on the Jackson.

Equipment to Use
Rods: 5-7 weight, 8-9 feet in length.
Reels: Standard mechanical.
Lines: Weight-forward floating, matched to rod. A sink tip will help in certain stretches.
Leaders: 4X-6X leaders, 9 feet in length.
Wading: Because of some pretty deep sections, stick to chest waders on the Jackson.

Flies to Use
Dries: Adams #14-20, BWO #14-20, Braided Butt Damsel #10-12, Dusty's Deviant #12-16, Elk Hair Caddis #14-20, Flying Ant #10-18, Gelso's Little Black Stonefly #16-20, Lt. Cahill #14-20, Little Yellow Sally #14-20, March Brown #10-14, Murray's Mr. Rapidan #14-20, Pale Morning Dun #14-20, Quill Gordon #12-22, Stimulator #12-20, Steeves' Attract Ant #16-20, Steeves' Bark Beetle #16-20, Steeves' Crystal Butt Hopper #8-10, Steeves' Disc O' Beetle #14, Steeves' UFO #10.
Nymphs & Streamers: Beadhead Goldilox #6-10, Beadhead Hare's Ear #14-20, Beadhead Prince Nymph #14-20, Bruce's Little Bow #6, Coburn's Cress Bug #14-20, Coburn's Inchworm #12-14, Dover's Peach Fly #6-10, Egg #6-20, Finn's Golden Retriever #6-10, Green Weenie #14-16, Matuka #4-10, Mickey Finn #6-10, MC2 Crayfish #4-6, Muddler Minnow #6-10, Pheasant Tail #14-20, River Witch #6, Scud #10-18, Sculpin #4-8, Woolly Bugger #6-10.

When to Fish
There are no bad times to fish the Jackson—any chance you have to get away and wet a line, you should. That said, April through November is best.

Season & Limits
There are put-and-take sections on the Jackson as well as the special regulation section in Hidden Valley on the upper section. Check for nearby signs posted on trees for the rules in the section you're fishing.

Nearby Fly Fishing
Alternatives include the upper Jackson above the Gathright Dam and Back Creek.

Accommodations & Services
Warm Springs is the nearest hamlet with all the basics. The closest fly shop is Allegheny Outfitters at The Homestead resort in Hot Springs. For a crack at some private water on the Jackson, stay at Meadow Lane Lodge (see "Private Waters", page 150).

Rating
The Jackson is a must-fish river. Allow yourself plenty of time to explore this outstanding trout water. The size and scenery combined with the quality of the trout translate to a rating of 9.

Use the river's current to make the movements of your pattern appear lifelike. Photo by Beau Beasley.

Much of the lower Jackson is posted, so be careful where you fish. Photo by Beau Beasley.

The moss that covers nearly all the rocks on the lower Jackson can make wading difficult. Photo by Beau Beasley.

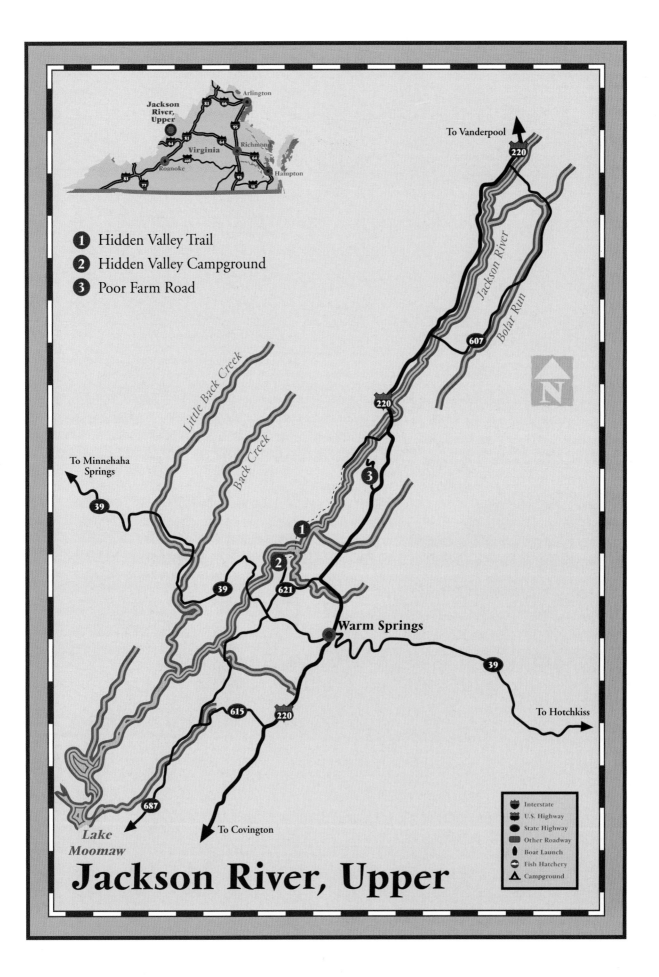

To Vanderpool

220

Jackson River

Bolar Run

607

220

Little Back Creek

Back Creek

To Minnehaha
Springs

39

1 Hidden Valley Trail
2 Hidden Valley Campground
3 Poor Farm Road

Jackson
River,
Upper

Arlington

Virginia

Richmond

Roanoke

Hampton

N

3

1

2

39

621

Warm Springs

39

To Hotchkiss

615

220

687

To Covington

*Lake
Moomaw*

Interstate
U.S. Highway
State Highway
Other Roadway
Boat Launch
Fish Hatchery
Campground

Jackson River, Upper

Jackson River
Upper Section

Jenny Hickey and King Montgomery with a nice rainbow. Photo courtesy of King Montgomery.

Few Virginia waters can rival the trout fishing on the Jackson River. The Jackson courses through Highland, Bath, and Alleghany Counties before it meets the Cowpasture River, creating the James River near Clifton Forge. Here is a river that trout-loving fly anglers can sink their teeth into without fear of shallow water or the tight canopy cover that is a fixture of most good trout streams. It helps to think of the Jackson in two parts: an upper and a lower section, with Lake Moomaw and the Gathright Dam being the line of demarcation between the two.

Much of the upper portion of the Jackson River runs through the George Washington and Jefferson National Forests—over land owned by the USDA Forest Service—and is therefore open to the public. There are also sections, however, that are posted, so be sure to look for signs before you start fishing.

Not far from the town of Warm Springs is an area known as Hidden Valley. This area, which has a nearby campground, boasts a 3-mile special regulation section. You will, however, have

The upper Jackson on a late summer's day. Photo by Beau Beasley.

Falling Springs, a tributary of the Jackson River, creates a beautiful waterfall near The Homestead resort. Photo by Beau Beasley.

to hike in to take advantage of this restricted fishing area, so go prepared to make a day of it. Many anglers make the mistake of carrying extra flies, back-up rods, and even extra reels, but forget to bring something to eat. Think ahead before you go. You may want to freeze a container of water and carry a good old fashioned peanut butter and jelly sandwich in with you.

By the way, there is an annual run of rainbow trout that venture out of Lake Moomaw in late winter and early spring. Land one of these fish and you are likely to behold a trout that exceeds five pounds—so you'll need that PB&J just to keep up your strength.

The Jackson is the rare Virginia trout stream: its breadth dwarfs that of many of the state's better-known trout waters. Most Virginians assume that the Jackson is named after the famous Confederate cavalry officer Stonewall Jackson—even some of the locals believe it—but this is incorrect. In fact the river was named after colonial-era landowner William Jackson, who in 1746 owned an enormous tract of land around the river.

Well worth a trip to the western region of the state, the Jackson is a trout angler's delight. Here you can watch your pattern as it drifts for yards at a time. Here you can easily cast 50 feet (assuming, of course, that you can cast that far) and have plenty of water to fight your fish. No tight cover here, just wide open water and plenty of it.

To reach the lower part of the special regulation section near Hidden Valley, take route 621 from route 39 and follow the Forest Service signs to Hidden Valley. Be sure to go past the campground and start your hike at the trail head. To reach the upper section of Hidden Valley, take 220 north from Warm Springs and turn left on Route 623 (Poor Farm Road), continuing until it ends in a small turnaround. Remember to take all the items with you that you'll need all day.

Rainbows and big browns are caught each year on the Jackson. Photo by Beau Beasley.

Types of Fish

You'll find mostly healthy rainbows here and you can also catch some nice browns. Don't be surprised if that tug you feel comes from the occasional brook trout because the surrounding feeder creeks support these wild fish.

Known Hatches

Blue Quills, Hendricksons, March Browns, Little Yellow Stoneflies, Sulfurs, Quill Gordons, Caddis, Cahills, inchworms, and terrestrials are major food components on the Jackson.

Equipment to Use

Rods: 5-7 weight, 8-9 feet in length.
Reels: Standard mechanical.
Lines: Weight-forward floating, matched to rod. A sink tip will help in certain stretches.
Leaders: 4X-6X leaders, 9 feet in length.
Wading: Because of some pretty deep sections, stick to chest waders on the Jackson.

Flies to Use

Dries: Adams #14-20, BWO #14-20, Braided Butt Damsel #10-12, Dusty's Deviant #12-16, Elk Hair Caddis #14-20, Flying Ant #10-18, Gelso's Little Black Stonefly #16-20, Lt. Cahill #14-20, Little Yellow Sally #14-20, March Brown #10-14, Murray's Mr. Rapidan #14-20, Pale Morning Dun #14-20, Quill Gordon #12-22, Stimulator #12-20, Steeves' Attract Ant #16-20, Steeves' Bark Beetle #16-20, Steeves' Crystal Butt Hopper #8-10, Steeves' Disc O' Beetle #14, Steeves' UFO #10. *Nymphs & Streamers:* BH Goldilox #6-10, BH Hare's Ear #14-20, BH Prince Nymph #14-20, Bruce's Little Bow #6, Coburn's Cress Bug #14-20, Coburn's Inchworm #12-14, Egg #6-20, Finn's Golden Retriever #6-10, Green Weenie #14-16, Matuka #4-10, Mickey Finn #6-10, MC2 Crayfish #4-6, Muddler Minnow #6-10, Murray's Marauder #6-10, Pheasant Tail #14-20, River Witch #6, Scud #10-18, Sculpin #4-8, Woolly Bugger #6-10.

When to Fish

The Jackson is a four-season fishery if ever there was one—there's no bad time to go. That said, spring and fall are the best.

Season & Limits

There are put-and-take sections on the Jackson as well as the special regulation section in Hidden Valley. Check for nearby signs posted on trees to let you know what the rules are in the section you are fishing. I encourage you to release all your fish.

Nearby Fly Fishing

Alternatives include the lower Jackson below the Gathright Dam and Back Creek.

Accommodations & Services

Warm Springs is the closest nearby hamlet where you can find all the basics. The closest fly shop, however, is Allegheny Outfitters at the luxurious Homestead resort in Hot Springs.

Rating

No matter the origin of its name, the Jackson ranks as one of the best rivers in the state. Its sheer size, breathtaking scenery, and hard-fighting fish contribute to a stellar rating of 9.

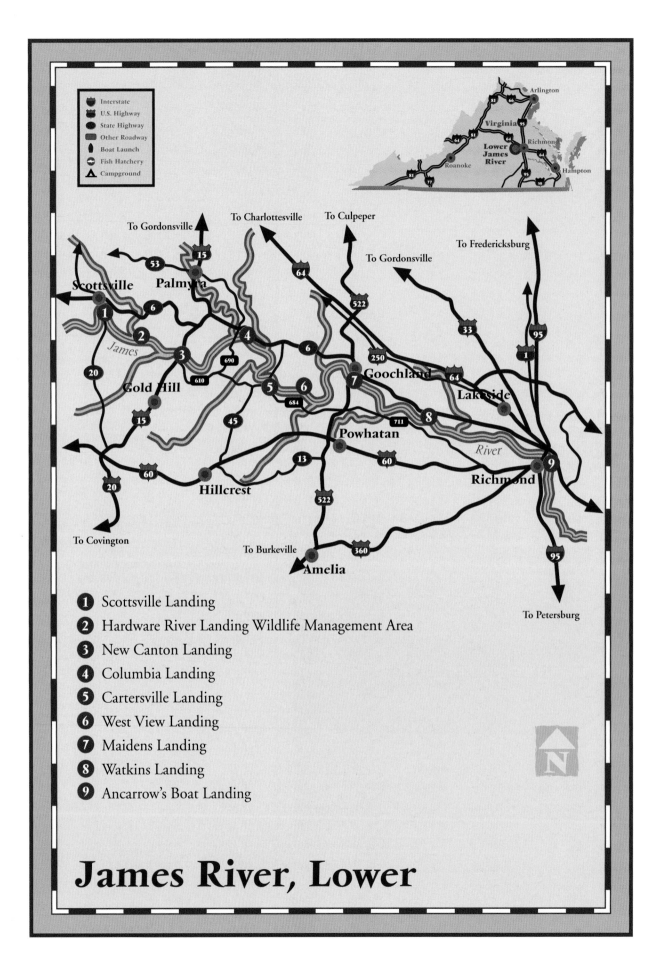

Legend:
- Interstate
- U.S. Highway
- State Highway
- Other Roadway
- Boat Launch
- Fish Hatchery
- Campground

To Gordonsville
To Charlottesville
To Culpeper
To Gordonsville
To Fredericksburg

53
15
Scottsville
Palmyra
6
James
64
522
33
95
1
690
4
6
250
Goochland
64
Lakeside
3
610
20
Gold Hill
5
6
7
15
684
8
711
River
45
Powhatan
13
60
9
Hillcrest
60
522
Richmond
20
To Covington
To Burkeville
360
95
Amelia
To Petersburg

Arlington
81 66
Virginia
95
64 81
Lower James River
Richmond
64
Roanoke
Hampton
81 77
95

1 Scottsville Landing
2 Hardware River Landing Wildlife Management Area
3 New Canton Landing
4 Columbia Landing
5 Cartersville Landing
6 West View Landing
7 Maidens Landing
8 Watkins Landing
9 Ancarrow's Boat Landing

N

James River, Lower

James River
Lower Section

The James is Virginia's largest and best-known river. Here anglers are fishing beneath the I-95 bridge in Richmond. Photo by Beau Beasley.

In 1607 Captain John Smith sailed as far up the James River as he could go. Reaching what is now the city of Richmond, rocks and turbulent waters at what we now refer to as the fall line forced Smith to turn back. In his diary Smith recorded that the fish were so thick on this water that he could scoop them up with a frying pan. Smith recognized that this was the largest river he had discovered thus far in the New World—and being an astute person as well as an intrepid explorer, he quickly named the river after His Majesty, King James I of England.

From Scottsville to the Ancarrow's landing just off of Maury Street and Interstate 95 in Richmond lies some of the best warm water fishing anyone could ever hope for. Shad start moving up the James in the late spring by the hundreds of thousands. In colonial times, the James River shad run was so large that farmers had to move cattle away from the water because the surging masses of fish would startle them and cause them to break down their fences. Hurrying the shad along are stripers, which also use the James as a spawning ground.

The James on a late summer's day. Photo by Beau Beasley.

Crappie in the lower James will readily take streamer patterns. Photo by King Montgomery.

By late May you can often drive along the James and see smallmouth bass and other fish literally jumping from the river to catch dragonflies that buzz along the top of the water like tiny airplanes. The James River dragonfly hatch is so strong that at times it appears that the top of the river takes on a blue haze owing to the massive cloud of these insects hovering over the water. Little wonder then that patterns like Hickey's Condor, Walt's Poppers, and Chocklett's Dragon Fly, which all come in blue, fly off the shelves of local fly shops at this time of year.

Perhaps the best way to approach the James for the first time is with a guide. A river this large can be intimidating. Spend the day with a guide who can give you the inside scoop on this water, and you won't regret it. The James is known for its rock ledges that act as ambush points for larger predators like smallmouth and muskie. But don't forget to cast to shady spots and the areas beneath the tree canopy with dragonfly imitations.

The James River is known across the nation as one of the best smallmouth bass fisheries on the East Coast. Anglers of all stripes flock here each season carrying everything from cane rods with red and white floats tied to the end of a string, to cane rods that cost as much as my first car (well, OK—*more* than my first car). For both the novice and the veteran fly angler, the majestic James River is a great place to wet a line.

Although the James is famous for its smallies and shad, you can also catch perch. Photo by Steve Probasco.

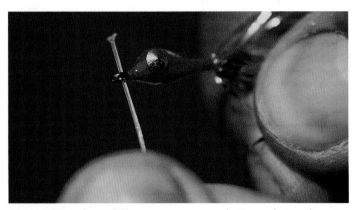

Tommy's Torpedo is a killer pattern to use on the James during the spring shad migration—though smallies and stripers will happily strike it as well. Photo by Steve Probasco.

Types of Fish

Smallmouth bass are sought after more than any other species on the James, but you can also catch largemouth bass, catfish, shad, perch, carp, gar, and crappie.

Known Hatches

Hatches on the James can be largely ignored by many of the fish because there is so much for them to eat. It's a safe bet however that beetles, crickets, and especially damselflies and dragonflies do come off in great numbers. Crayfish, frogs, hellgrammites, as well as various baitfishes like sculpins and madtoms are prolific on this river.

Equipment to Use

Rods: 6-9 weight, 8 to 9½ feet in length.
Reels: Mechanical and palm.
Lines: Weight-forward floating matched to rod. Sink tips will work in some places. Sinking lines in the 200- to 300-grain range work best for shad and stripers.
Leaders: 2X-5X leaders, 9 feet in length.
Wading: Anglers have the option of floating this river in several locations. Chest waders are another option as is wet wading.

Flies to Use

For shad and stripers try Mohnsen's Buggit #6-8, Simmons' Shad Fly #4-6, Tommy's Flash Torpedo #4-6, Tommy's Torpedo #4-6, Bruce's Bay Anchovy #2, Clouser Minnow #2/0-4, DuBiel's Finesse Fly #2-4, DuBiel's Lil'haden #1/0-2, DuBiel's Red-Ducer #1/0-2, Lefty's Deceiver #2/0-2, Lefty's Half and Half, #2/0-2, Tommy's Eel Fly #2/0-1/0, Trow's Minnow #2/0-6. For all other fish, BH Goldilox #4-8, Bruce's Little Bow #2-6, Chocklett's Disc Slider #1/0, Chocklett's Gummy Minnow #6, CK Baitfish #1, Claw-Dad #2-6, Clouser Minnow #1/0-6, Cramer's Jail Bait Minnow #2-4, Finn's Golden Retriever #6-10, Hansen's Electric Frog #6, Hickey's Condor #6-12, Kreelex #2-6, MC2 Crayfish #4-6, Murray's Lead Eye Hellgrammite #6, Murray's Marauder #6, Patuxent Special #6-10, San Antonio Worm #4, Shenk's White Minnow #4-6, Super Patuxent Special #6-10, Trow's Minnow #1/0-6, Walt's Popper #2-12.

When to Fish

The James River fishes well nearly all year. American shad as well as herring and stripers start to show up in the river in late March and continue through late April. From late April through the fall, anglers will find great bass fishing all along this wonderful river.

Season & Limits

Open all year.

Nearby Fly Fishing

Other nearby fisheries include the Rappahannock River and the lower Rapidan.

Accommodations & Services

The lower James River runs along several cities, most notably Richmond. The state capital is home to numerous lodging and dining options, from the most humble to the most lavish imaginable.

Rating

Considering the variety of fish one can catch on the James as well as its many access points, the James River rates a 9.

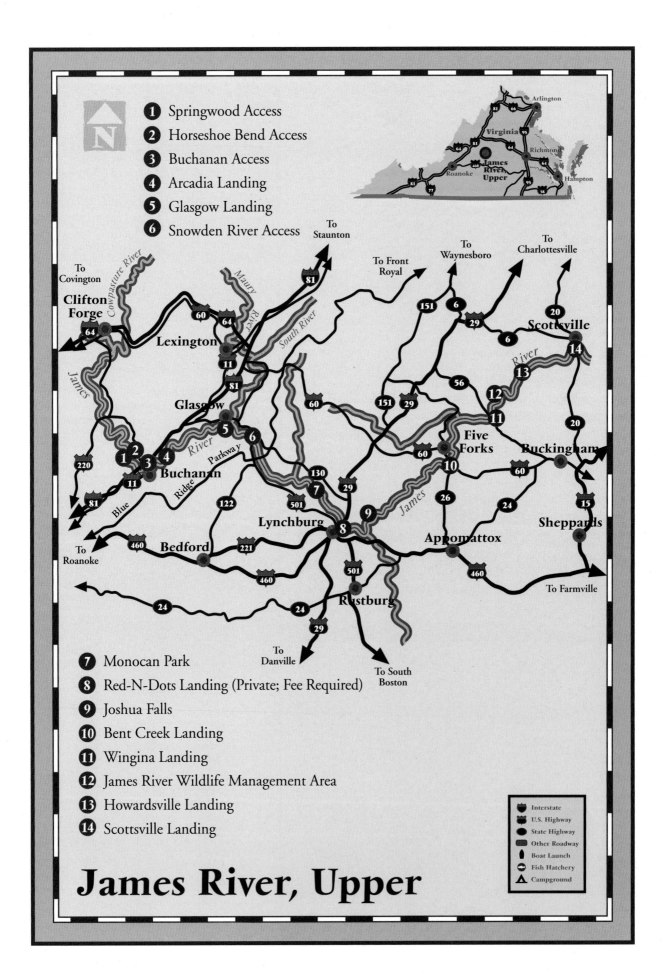

N

1 Springwood Access
2 Horseshoe Bend Access
3 Buchanan Access
4 Arcadia Landing
5 Glasgow Landing
6 Snowden River Access

7 Monocan Park
8 Red-N-Dots Landing (Private; Fee Required)
9 Joshua Falls
10 Bent Creek Landing
11 Wingina Landing
12 James River Wildlife Management Area
13 Howardsville Landing
14 Scottsville Landing

Interstate	
U.S. Highway	
State Highway	
Other Roadway	
Boat Launch	
Fish Hatchery	
Campground	

James River, Upper

James River
Upper Section

The headwaters of Virginia's venerable James River begin in the mountains of western Virginia where the Jackson and the Cowpasture rivers meet near Iron Gate. As the best-known river in the state, the James draws spin and fly anglers from across the country. Enthusiasts have written entire books on the history and fishability of the James River—I can't possibly do it justice in this space, even by breaking the river down into its upper and lower sections. Nevertheless, let us consider the upper James to be that stretch that runs from Iron Gate to Scottsville. Anglers will find hundreds of places to wet a line in just this section of river by canoeing or wading in public parks.

Even breaking the James down into upper and lower sections may leave anglers feeling a bit overwhelmed. To make things easier, break it down further from Iron Gate to Lynchburg and from there to Scottsville. The area between Iron Gate and Lynchburg is more mountainous. The water is swifter here because the river has cut steep, cavernous sections from the sides of the mountains. The uppermost section of the James from Iron Gate to Lynchburg is also where you are more

L. E. Rhodes of Hatch Matcher Guide Service has been fishing on the James River since childhood. Photo by Beau Beasley.

Bluegill on the James can grow quite large. Photo by King Montgomery.

First light on the James: prime time to fish.
Photo by King Montgomery.

likely to catch muskellunge. These fish, the largest member of the pike family, can grow beyond 40 inches in length and are tremendous predators. Anglers hoping to land muskellunge should be prepared to cast 2/0-3/0 flies with wire leaders and work them in deep water near structure. Such fishing can be slow going—but if you are good and patient enough to actually land a muskellunge, you're in for a heck of a fight.

From Lynchburg to Scottsville the water slows down a bit and spreads out, with river banks that are a bit wider than the section above. Considered the piedmont section of the James, this stretch offers wading anglers a bit more access. You'll also find good wading in Lynchburg itself at Percival's Island. The knowledgeable staffers at Angler's Lane in Lynchburg can help anglers find these key access points. They also offer a guide service for the upper section of the James River.

For those wishing to float the James with a guide or on their own, there are variety of float trips to choose from ranging from just over two miles to 15 miles and everything in between. A number of boat ramps line the river, some with concrete ramps that allow you to back a trailer right into the river, and others that are much smaller and more appropriate for those using kayaks or canoes. I'd suggest that James River novices explore the upper sections of the river by hiring a guide—or at the very least, spend a little time checking the water out from a boat before fishing—simply because this is vast water.

The blue damsel hatch on the James River is well known. This is the main reason the color blue works so well on this river. Photo by Beau Beasley.

Types of Fish
Smallies are king on the upper James. Anglers may also catch rock bass, carp, catfish, and the occasional muskellunge. Although rare, anglers have even caught a few trout that have been swept downstream after floods (from the good trout water that feeds the James).

Known Hatches
The James boasts all sorts of hatches—most of which go ignored by the local warm water fish. Dragonflies are a significant food source on the James as are beetles, spiders, and crickets. Two other important sources of food are crayfish and minnows, so consider throwing plenty of patterns that mimic these river dwellers.

Equipment to Use
Rods: 6-9 weight, 8-9½ feet in length.
Reels: Standard mechanical unless you are fishing for Muskie. In this case you will need a large arbor reel and plenty of 30lb test backing.
Lines: Weight-forward floating, matched to rod. Sink tips work as well.
Leaders: 1X-3X leaders, 9 feet in length, wire leaders will be needed for Muskie fishing.
Wading: Boating is a great way to fish the upper James. Also try kayaking or canoeing in conjunction with chest waders, and fish the banks and small islands as well.

Flies to Use
BH Goldilox #4-8, Claw-Dad #2-6, Chocklett's Disc Slider #1/0, Chocklett's Gummy Minnow #6, CK Baitfish #1, Clouser Minnow #1/0-6, Cramer's Jail Bait Minnow #2-4, Dover's Peach Fly #6-10, Finn's Golden Retriever #6-10, Hansen's Electric Frog #6, Hickey's Condor #6-12, Kreelex #2-6, MC2 Crayfish #4-6, Murray's Lead Eye Hellgrammite #6, Murray's Marauder #6, San Antonio Worm #4, Shenk's White Minnow #4-6, Super Patuxent Special #6-10, Trow's Minnow #1/0-6, Walt's Popper #2-12.

When to Fish
As in most Virginia waters, fishing in the James depends on the weather. March can be good if you fish slow and deep. Nevertheless it is May before the fish really start to move. From June until late fall, James River fishing can be red hot.

Season & Limits
The James is open all year. Check local game laws for specific species limits.

Nearby Fly Fishing
Alternative fishing locales include the Jackson River and Back Creek as well as parts of the Shenandoah National Park.

Accommodations & Services
Consider Lynchburg, Roanoke, or Charlottesville as a base of operations when fishing the upper James. Each city has plenty of lodging and dining options, and each supports a fly shop. I recommend calling one of these shops to get the latest on James River fishing before you hit the water.

Rating
The upper James is a no-brainer, must-do fishery and easily rates a 9.

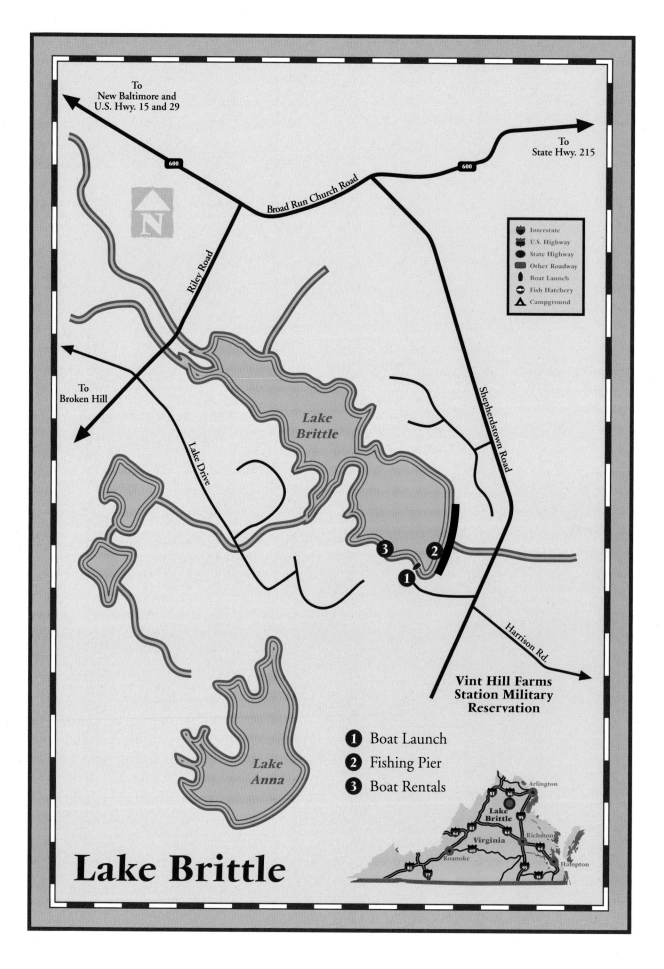

To
New Baltimore and
U.S. Hwy. 15 and 29

To
State Hwy. 215

600

600

Broad Run Church Road

Riley Road

N

Interstate
U.S. Highway
State Highway
Other Roadway
Boat Launch
Fish Hatchery
Campground

To
Broken Hill

Lake Brittle

Lake Drive

Shepherdstown Road

❸

❷

❶

Harrison Rd

Vint Hill Farms Station Military Reservation

Lake Anna

❶ Boat Launch
❷ Fishing Pier
❸ Boat Rentals

Arlington

Lake
Brittle

Richmond

Virginia

Roanoke

Hampton

Lake Brittle

Lake Brittle

Perhaps the best way to describe Lake Brittle is that you'll find it hiding out in the open. At the eastern end of bucolic but rapidly developing Fauquier County, Virginia, and lying right in between Gainesville and Warrenton off of busy Route 29, Lake Brittle offers easy access to a variety of warm water fish for those willing to take the plunge. It's often bypassed by anglers headed to the Shenandoah National Park and other better known waters. This leaves Lake Brittle nearly devoid of other anglers during the week and hence is a great way to blow a summer afternoon. And stopping here saves residents of Northern Virginia an hour's drive each way to and from the Shenandoah National Park. For these reasons alone, those looking for a warm water fishing alternative might want to check out Lake Brittle.

Lake Brittle is one of the oldest impoundments owned by the Virginia Department of Game and Inland Fisheries (VDGIF). Built in 1953, this 77-acre lake is a fine example of tax dollars at work. The money to build it came from the Dingell-Johnson revenue, a fund set up to collect federal excise taxes on fishing tackle. (And you thought that the government wasn't here to help you!) On average Lake Brittle is seven feet deep, but it exceeds 20 feet in depth near the spillway tower at the northern end of the lake.

This bluegill fell for a Goddard Caddis.
Photo by King Montgomery.

Lake Brittle is a family-friendly, 24-hour-a-day fishery.
Photo by Beau Beasley.

Lake Brittle in the fall. Photo by Beau Beasley.

FISHING LIMITED TO SHORELINE AREA
PLEASE DO NOT TRESPASS
ON PRIVATE PROPERTY
BOUNDARY MARKED BY YELLOW
STRIPES ON TREES.

A sign near the entrance to Lake Brittle encourages anglers to stay close to the lake.
Photo by Beau Beasley.

A boat launch is available here near the anglers' parking lot, but only trolling motors are allowed. If you want to bring your kayak, feel free. This is the perfect place to get some practice before hitting rough water on the river. You can also rent a small johnboat with a trolling motor or use the fishing pier. The fishing pier has wooden railings, concrete flooring, and a partially covered area complete with roof. Though the pier is not practical for fly anglers, it's the perfect place to introduce Junior to fishing when he's just old enough to hold a conventional rod. There are even staggered railings so that children under ten can hold rods themselves without fear of falling into the water.

Though you may not wade into the lake, those unwilling to rent a boat will find plenty of access from the northern section of the lake. A 300-yard-long embankment flanks the north side of the lake without pesky trees, which allows fly anglers to cast from the shoreline. A word of warning, however: the tall grass on the banks looks as hungry for your fly as the fish you're attempting to cast to, and it also looks like an inviting place for a snake to take a nap.

You won't catch species like trout here, but you've got a good chance of landing some decent-sized walleye, which can exceed four pounds. If popping bugs and bluegill are your game, come prepared to take on the big boys: bluegill in Lake Brittle often tip the scale at two pounds. And quite frankly, just the thought of catching a two-pound bluegill around the corner from my house is enough to make me have second thoughts about heading off on a long, winding excursion in search of finicky mountain trout.

Lake Brittle is managed by the VDGIF and is open to fishing 24 hours a day. Photo by Beau Beasley.

Types of Fish

Most anglers come for the largemouth bass, but you'll find sunfish as well as walleye (which were introduced to Lake Brittle to keep the levels of sunfish and gizzard shad in check).

Known Hatches and Baitfish

Consistent with what you'll find in other warm water impoundments; dragonflies and other terrestrials, frogs, and small baitfish.

Equipment to Use

Rods: 4-8 weight, 8-9 feet in length.
Reels: Mechanical and palm.
Lines: Weight-forward floating matched to rod. You could also use sink tips.
Leaders: 3X-5X, 9 feet in length.
Wading: Limited shore access. Your best bet is a boat. You can also launch your own canoe, kayak, or float tube.

Flies to Use

BH Goldilox #4-8, Bruce's Little Bow #2-6, Chocklett's Gummy Minnow #6, CK Baitfish #1, Claw-Dad #2-6, Clouser Minnow #2-6, Cramer's Jail Bait Minnow #2-4, Finn's Golden Retriever #6-10, Hansen's Electric Frog #6, Hickey's Condor #6-12, Kreelex #2-6, MC2 Crayfish #4-6, Murray's Lead Eye Hellgrammite #6, Murray's Marauder #6, Patuxent Special #6-10, San Antonio Worm #4, Shenk's White Minnow #4-6, Super Patuxent Special #6-10, Trow's Minnow #2-6, Walt's Popper #2-12.

When to Fish

Lake Brittle can be fished year-round, but don't expect much action until late April—after which, you'll find good fishing until the crisp fall weather puts the brakes on the fish.

Season & Limits

Check with local game laws concerning creel limits. Lake Brittle is one of the few places where you can fish 24 hours a day, so if you'd like to try your hand at night fishing with a fly rod, try it here.

Nearby Fly Fishing

Alternatives include the lower Rapidan and the upper reaches of the Rappahannock. You can also drive an hour farther south on Route 29 and have good access to the fishing in the Shenandoah National Park.

Accommodations & Services

Anglers will find lodging and dining options in nearby Gainesville, Haymarket, and Warrenton. Of the three, only Warrenton can boast a full-service fly shop: Rhodes Fly Shop on Main Street.

Rating

Lake Brittle is rated a 7.

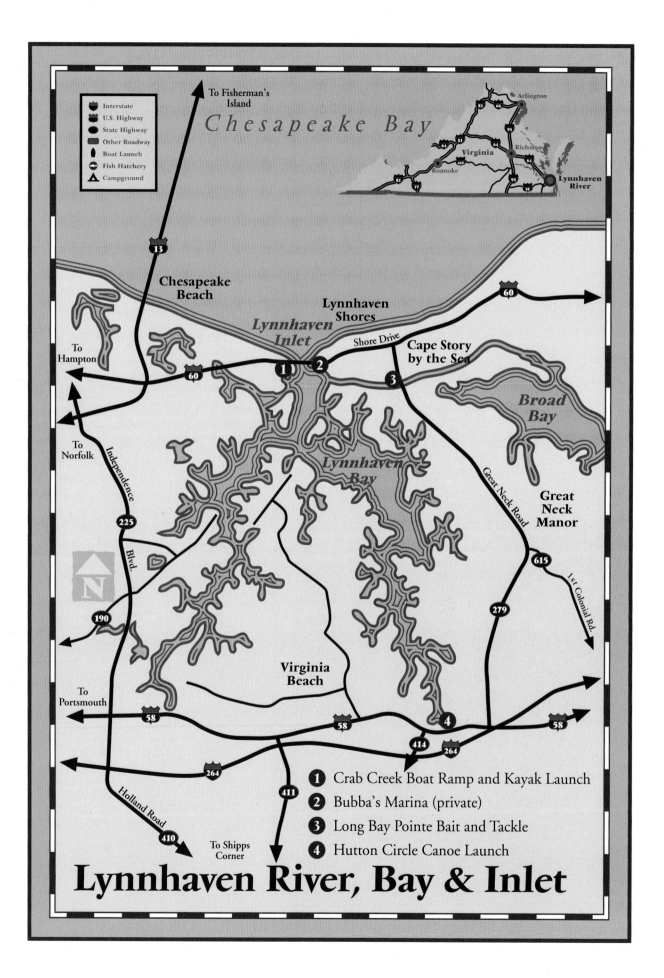

Lynnhaven River, Bay & Inlet

Legend:
- Interstate
- U.S. Highway
- State Highway
- Other Roadway
- Boat Launch
- Fish Hatchery
- Campground

Chesapeake Bay

Arlington
Virginia
Richmond
Roanoke
Lynnhaven River

To Fisherman's Island

Chesapeake Beach

Lynnhaven Shores

Lynnhaven Inlet

Shore Drive

Cape Story by the Sea

Broad Bay

To Hampton

To Norfolk

Independence Blvd.

Lynnhaven Bay

Great Neck Road

Great Neck Manor

1st Colonial Rd.

To Portsmouth

Virginia Beach

Holland Road

To Shipps Corner

1. Crab Creek Boat Ramp and Kayak Launch
2. Bubba's Marina (private)
3. Long Bay Pointe Bait and Tackle
4. Hutton Circle Canoe Launch

Lynnhaven River, Bay, & Inlet

I love to drive over the Lisner Bridge with my windows down. This way I can smell the salty sea breezes while I drive. And I always strain to see if I can identify birds working in the distance, no doubt feeding on small baitfish that hungry stripers or blues are pushing up from below. Below the bridge the Lynnhaven River, which ultimately feeds into Lynnhaven Bay and then becomes Lynnhaven Inlet, encompasses 64 square miles of saltwater and offers anglers more than 120 miles of shoreline.

The Lynnhaven has a rich and colorful history. During the 1600s, the Chesapeake Bay was terrorized by well-armed pirate ships. Virginia merchant ships would congregate together at Lynnhaven Inlet and then sail under convoy rather than brave the seas alone. During the Revolutionary War, French and British gunships fought fiercely here. The French managed to force the British Navy to retreat, sending British General Cornwallis to regroup in a little-known Virginia hamlet named Yorktown.

Captain Cory Routh is the Lynnhaven estuary's resident expert. He's fished these waters all his life and knows them as only a local can. "This area is like a miniature Chesapeake Bay," he says, "except that it's better protected from the wind. It's also

Captain Cory Routh fishing near the docks at Lynnhaven Marina. Photo by Steve Probasco.

Fly and light tackle anglers like to use kayaks for better access. This angler is fishing near the Lisner Bridge. Photo by Beau Beasley.

Captain Cory Routh knows the Lynnhaven River well and is a pioneer of saltwater fly fishing from a kayak. Photo by Steve Probasco.

easier to get to than boating all the way out to the islands. I sometimes laugh when I see guys heading out for the deeper parts of the Bay because I know what an incredible fishery this is."

An advantage to fishing the Lynnhaven is the fact that most of the area is readily accessible by boat in a short period of time, which is great for time-starved anglers and those who have hired a guide for only half a day. Routh has developed a thriving guide service taking anglers out in kayaks, which enables them to reach parts of the inlet—like inviting sandbars—that would be impossible to access from a traditional boat. If you have your own kayak, just put in at one of the public docks and get to fishing.

The first time you fish the Lynnhaven, you may be surprised by all of the surrounding development. At first blush all those houses may be off putting, but there's a silver lining: anglers who go out at night will find great fishing around homeowners' docks. The dock lights attract baitfish, which in turn attract larger predators. One evening Routh and I stopped fishing and just watched as stripers and small drum charged the baitfish in the water just below the dock lights. We then proceeded to do battle with these brutes by sight fishing for them with the aid of the dock lights.

The author with a nice drum caught near Lynnhaven Inlet. This fish fell for a Beadhead Goldilox, a fresh water trout fly. Photo by Steve Probasco.

Types of Fish
Lynnhaven offers anglers many choices, including stripers, bluefish, spot, speckled trout, flounder, croaker, and puppy drum.

Known Baitfish
Anglers fishing in and around Lynnhaven can expect to see shad, menhaden, shrimp, squid, crabs, a variety of small baitfish, and eels.

Equipment to Use
Rods: 6-9 weight rods, 9 to 9½ feet in length.
Reels: Mechanical and large arbor reels.
Lines: Fast to intermediate sink tips matched to rod, as well as sinking lines of 200-300 grains.
Leaders: 0X-2X leaders, 9 feet in length (wire leaders should be used if fishing for blues).
Wading: Anglers can use chest waders as well as canoes, kayaks, and boats.

Flies to Use
Bruce's Bay Anchovie #2, Bruce's Crystal Shrimp #1/0, Clouser Minnow #2/0-4, DuBiel's Finesse Fly #2-4, DuBiel's Lil'hadden #1/0-2, DuBiel's Red-Ducer #1/0-2, Lefty's Deceiver #2/0-2, Lefty's Half and Half, #2/0-2, Russell's Mussel #1/0-1, Tommy's Crease Fly #2/0-2, Tommy's Eel Fly #2/0-1/0, Trow's Minnow Saltwater #3/0-6.

When to Fish
The Lynnhaven is like a nursery for all manner of saltwater fish. Although spring and fall are prime times, you can go out on this river nearly any day of the year and catch fish.

Season & Limits
Open all year. Limits and sizes will depend on species and the time of year you're fishing.

Nearby Fly Fishing
The islands on the Chesapeake Bay and Rudee Inlet are other nearby saltwater options.

Accommodations & Services
There are abundant services nearby in Virginia Beach. Long Bay Pointe Bait & Tackle, adjacent to the Lynnhaven River, is primarily a conventional tackle store that also sells a limited amount of fly fishing gear.

Rating
The Lynnhaven estuary—river, bay, and inlet—holds a fond place in my heart as I have fished here often. Easily accessible and home to a wide variety of fish, the Lynnhaven easily rates an 8.

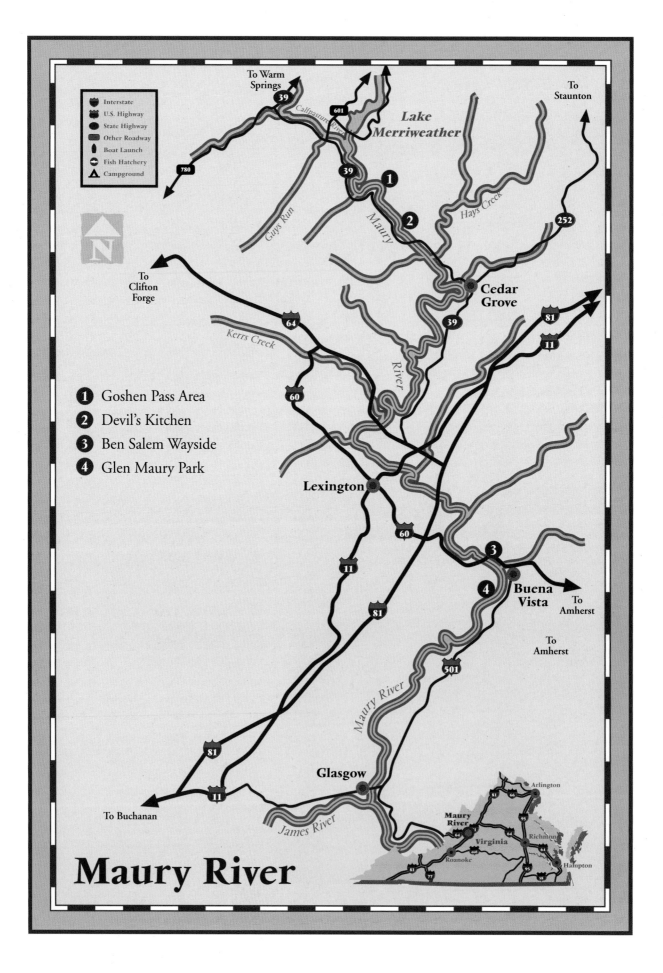

1 Goshen Pass Area
2 Devil's Kitchen
3 Ben Salem Wayside
4 Glen Maury Park

Legend:
- Interstate
- U.S. Highway
- State Highway
- Other Roadway
- Boat Launch
- Fish Hatchery
- Campground

To Warm Springs
To Staunton
Lake Merriweather
Hays Creek
Calfpasture River
Maury
Guys Run
39
601
780
39
39
252
1
2
Cedar Grove
To Clifton Forge
Kerrs Creek
64
60
River
39
81
11
N
Lexington
60
11
81
3
4
Buena Vista
To Amherst
To Amherst
501
81
Glasgow
James River
81
11
To Buchanan
Maury River

Maury River

Arlington
Maury River
Virginia
Richmond
Hampton
Roanoke

Maury River

Originally named the North River of the James because it flows into the James from the north, the Maury River courses across Rockbridge County for approximately 30 miles, passing through Lexington and Buena Vista and a part of the state steeped in history and heritage. The river was renamed for Matthew Fontaine Maury, a professor at Lexington's Virginia Military Institute who had distinguished himself as an oceanographer and had served in the Confederate forces. Maury fell in love with the river and asked that upon his death his remains be carried through the dramatic Goshen Pass and on to Richmond for burial. A small monument exists to honor him near the point at which a VMI honor guard carried his remains through Goshen Pass, according to his wishes.

Anglers might think of the Maury as having an upper and a lower section. You'll find easy access to the upper section from Route 39, though you must carefully negotiate the rocks to wade. The upper Maury is popular with spin fishermen, swimmers, and kayakers. Whitewater enthusiasts love its wild tumbles and rapids. This is a big river and moving up or down a few hundred yards should give you plenty of elbow room if you find yourself in close quarters. Fly anglers take note: the Maury's wide-open spaces make casting easy, long pools and deep plunge pools abound, and you'll find plenty of areas for fish to hide among

An angler fishing off the rocks of the Maury River. Photo by Beau Beasley.

The Goshen Pass area just off Rt. 39 is popular with kayakers as well as anglers. Photo by Beau Beasley.

The Maury River has both fast water and large, quiet stretches.
Photo by Beau Beasley.

the rocks that litter the river bottom. But wade carefully here because the swift water can easily sweep the careless downstream. A close-by area of whitewater called Devil's Kitchen provides a clue to the character of this part of the river.

The Maury's lower section, accessible near the Ben Salem Wayside area off of Rt. 60, slows considerably because of dams, giving the river a lethargic and even lazy look. Near the Ben Salem Wayside area, explorers will find remnants of old stone locks and canals dating from George Washington's presidency. His plan had been to increase trade through the upper section of the state by getting goods to the James River quickly. The railroad era brought this endeavor to an end.

Easily accessible from Interstate 81 and Rt. 60 with multiple entry points and with excellent camping facilities available near Buena Vista, the Maury holds promise for anglers as well as other outdoor enthusiasts. The real question, then, becomes, what shall I fish for? The state stocks both rainbows and browns, and the river supports a healthy resident smallmouth population (as well as other assorted sunfish). So bring your canoe or kayak and enjoy both the thrill and the calm of Maury's beloved waters.

Remnants of a stone canal near the Ben Salem Wayside. The canal system was abandoned after the advent of the railroad. Photo by Beau Beasley.

Types of Fish

The Maury holds a wide variety of fish, including stocked rainbow and brown trout as well as smallmouth bass, bluegill, carp, and rock bass.

Known Hatches

Hatches on the Maury are a mixed bag because it is both a cold and warm water fishery depending on where you are on the river. In the upper portion near Route 39 you can expect to see Blue Quill, Hendrickson, March Browns, Sulfurs, Caddis, Cahills, inchworms, and other terrestrials. You'll also find a large population of varied baitfish here.

Equipment to Use

Rods: 4-7 weight, 7½-9 feet in length.
Reels: Mechanical and palm.
Lines: Weight-forward floating, matched to rod.
Leaders: 4X-5X leaders, 9 feet in length.
Wading: Hip waders are fine here.

Flies to Use

Dries: Adams #14-20, Braided Butt Damsel #10-12, BWO #14-20, Dusty's Deviant #12-16, Elk Hair Caddis #14-20, Flying Ant #10-18, Gelso's Little Black Stonefly #16-20, Lt. Cahill #14-20, Little Yellow Sally #14-20, March Brown #10-14, Murray's Mr. Rapidan #14-20, Pale Morning Dun #14-20, Quill Gordon #12-22, Steeves' Attract Ant #16-20, Steeves' Bark Beetle #16-20, Steeves' Crystal Butt Cricket #8-10, Steeves' Disc O' Beetle #14, Steeves' UFO #10, Stimulator #12-20.
Nymphs & Streamers: BH Goldilox #6-10, BH Hare's Ear #14-20, BH Prince Nymph #14-20, Bruce's Little Bow #6, Coburn's Cress Bug #14-20, Coburn's Inchworm #12-14, Egg #6-20, Finn's Golden Retriever #6-10, Green Weenie #14-16, Matuka #4-10, Mickey Finn #6-10, MC2 Crayfish #4-6, Muddler Minnow #6-10, Murray's Marauder #6-10, Pheasant Tail #14-20, River Witch #6, Scud #10-18, Sculpin #4-8, Woolly Bugger #6-10.

Other good surface patterns for bass would include Hansen's Electric Frog #6, Hickey's Condor #6-10, and Walt's Poppers #2-12.

When to Fish

You can fish here all year. I've had locals tell me that they like to fish for trout on the Maury from November through March because of the reduced pressure. The Maury is generally fished from April through October.

Season & Limits

The Maury is open to fishing all year. Check with local game laws to see which species can be creeled.

Nearby Fly Fishing

Alternative waters include the Rivanna, James, and Shenandoah Rivers as well as trout fishing in the Shenandoah National Park.

Accommodations & Services

Nearby Lexington, home to the Virginia Military Institute (VMI), has plenty to offer fly anglers in terms of dining and lodging. Unfortunately the only fly shop that serviced this city has closed.

Rating

Although the fish in the Maury aren't huge, the variety is impressive. I rate the Maury River a 7.

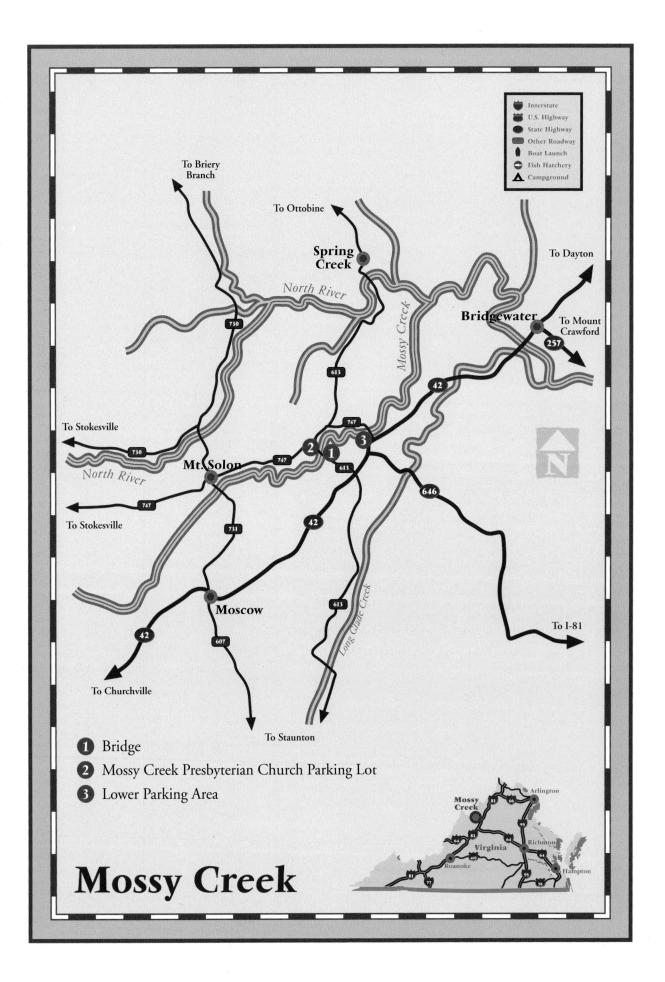

Mossy Creek

Legend:
- Interstate
- U.S. Highway
- State Highway
- Other Roadway
- Boat Launch
- Fish Hatchery
- Campground

To Briery Branch

To Ottobine

To Dayton

Spring Creek

North River

To Mount Crawford

Bridgewater

257

730

613

42

747

To Stokesville

730

747

2 1 3

747

613

Mt. Solon

747

646

42

731

N

To Stokesville

Moscow

42

613

To I-81

Long Glade Creek

42

607

To Churchville

To Staunton

1 Bridge
2 Mossy Creek Presbyterian Church Parking Lot
3 Lower Parking Area

Mossy Creek

Mossy Creek

Arlington

81 66

Virginia

64 95 Richmond

Roanoke

Hampton

77 95

Mossy Creek

Outdoor writer Dan Genest once described Mossy Creek to me as "an enigma meandering through a meadow"—and to date, his is the best description I've ever heard of this water. Mossy, as it is lovingly referred to by fly anglers in the Old Dominion, is arguably the most famous trout stream in Virginia, and with good reason. Anglers regularly catch trout in the 20-inch range here, as well as fish that exceed six pounds.

About a three-hour drive from the nation's capital, Mossy Creek runs through the picturesque Shenandoah Valley, what was once the heart of the Confederacy during the Civil War. Conveniently accessible from Interstate 81 near the hamlet of Bridgewater, Mossy sees visitors from around the country—and, in fact, the globe. Upon seeing Mossy for the first time, one might wonder why anyone would travel hundreds or even thousands of miles to fish here, in what amounts to an ordinary-looking spring creek. The answer is quite simple, really: Mossy's monster trout give new meaning to the term "selective." If anglers can make it here, they can make it almost anywhere.

Types of Fish
The river is famous for its big browns.

Known Hatches
The hatches on Mossy are consistent with what you would expect to find in most mountain streams. They include Blue Wing Olives, Winter Stoneflies, Blue Quills, Hendricksons, March Browns, Little Yellow Stoneflies, Sulfurs, Quill Gordons, Caddis, Cahills, and a host of terrestrials. This stream can also have a huge trico and midge hatch.

Equipment to Use
Rods: 3-8 weight, 7-9 feet in length.
Reels: Standard mechanical.
Lines: Weight-forward floating matched to rod. Use of the occasional sink tip is also an option.
Leaders: 2X-7X, 9-12 feet in length. The wide range is warranted due to the varying sizes of trout and the wide range of tactics employed on this beautiful but difficult stream.
Wading: Hip waders are fine, but anglers may not enter the river at any time.

Continued

Lefty Kreh releases a nice rainbow trout while friend Billy Kingsley looks on. Photo by King Montgomery.

Mossy Creek is by far the best known public trophy trout water in the state. This photo shows how the creek's rich vegetation provides its name. Photo by Beau Beasley.

The headwaters of Mossy Creek begin on Mount Solon, from which the river zigzags erratically like a drunken sailor across farmers' fields and private lands for nearly seven miles before it empties into the North River. Although Mossy flows through both Rockingham and Augusta counties, it's the three mile stretch of fly-fishing-only water in Augusta County that draws the attention of most fly anglers. This Special Regulation Trophy Trout Stream is surrounded by privately owned land, and if not for the consideration of the landowners, this jewel of the Commonwealth would remain out of reach of most anglers.

Fishing Mossy Creek is not for the weak. Although there are few trees to grab your fly, there is also little room for mistakes here. Drag-free drifts and delicate presentations are the order of the day. The funny thing is, it's also the place for plopping large leggy-type flies and trolling six-inch streamers along undercut banks and near heavy vegetation. Anglers can use a wide variety of fishing techniques on Mossy and the key to success is patience and experience. Although you will be tempted to fish beneath the bridge near the parking area, these trout have seen more fly anglers than you have, so move on either above the bridge or below. The barbed wire fencing looks menacing, but new wooden fence crossings were added in 2005, making trips in and out of the creek much easier and safer.

Fly anglers owe much to the efforts of conservationists—particularly Virginia Department of Game and Inland Fisheries biologist Larry Mohn and Shenandoah Valley Trout Unlimited member Urbie Nash—who convinced local landowners to fence out their cattle in exchange for state stocking of the stream. These tireless individuals also built up Mossy with riparian grasses and stream bank structure. The combined efforts of private landowners, state officials, and local Trout Unlimited chapters and members have made Mossy Creek the envy of trout anglers across the Mid-Atlantic region.

Colby Trow with a hard-won Mossy Creek brown trout.
Photo by Brian Trow.

Flies to Use

Dries: Adams #14-20, Braided Butt Damsel #10-12, BWO #14-20, Dusty's Deviant #12-16, Elk Hair Caddis #14-20, Flying Ant #10-18, Gelso's Little Black Stonefly #16-20, Lt. Cahill #14-20, Little Yellow Sally #14-20, March Brown #10-14, Murray's Mr. Rapidan #14-20, Pale Morning Dun #14-20, Quill Gordon #12-22, Stimulator #12-20, Steeves' Attract Ant #16-20, Steeves' Bark Beetle #16-20, Steeves' Crystal Butt Cricket #8-10, Steeves' Disc O' Beetle #14, Steeves' UFO #10.

Nymphs & Streamers: BH Goldilox #6-10, BH Hare's Ear #14-20, BH Prince Nymph #14-20, Bruce's Little Bow #6, Coburn's Cress Bug #14-20, Coburn's Inchworm #12-14, Egg #6-20, Finn's Golden Retriever #6-10, Green Weenie #14-16, Matuka #4-10, Mickey Finn #6-10, MC2 Crayfish #4-6, Muddler Minnow #6-10, Murray's Marauder #6-10, Pheasant Tail #14-20, River Witch #6, Scud #10-18, Sculpin #4-8, Woolly Bugger #6-10.

Keep in mind that the larger fish will often hit patterns much larger than you would normally consider for trout. With that in mind, don't be afraid to throw large streamers near undercut banks. These additional patterns would include Cramer's Jail Bait, Kraft's Claw-Dad and Kreelex as well as Trow's Minnow, Tommy's Eel Fly, and assorted deer hair bass bugs in sizes #1/0-2.

When to Fish

You'll never find a bad time to fish Mossy Creek. The stream is spring fed, so most of the time the water stays at about 56-60 degrees. The water can be low in the summer—but this doesn't keep the fish from biting. Keep in mind that if you want to focus on the larger trout, you'll need to use tactics and flies more akin to catching smallies than trout.

Seasons & Limits

Mossy Creek is a fly-fishing-only stream. Anglers may keep one fish over 18 inches. If you do, however, I personally believe that you should be summarily shot! You will need a special permit from the landowners and VDGIF to fish the public-access section of Mossy Creek. Send a self-addressed, stamped envelope to VDGIF, Verona Office, P.O. Box 996, Verona, VA 24482. The permit, good for a year, is free.

Nearby Fly Fishing

Keep in mind this stream also has private water; several guides have access to those private sections on Mossy. You may do well to hire a guide for one day and fish the public section the next. Other nearby fishing opportunities include the St. Mary's, the South River, and other portions of the Shenandoah National Park.

Accommodations & Services

Bridgewater is near Mossy Creek. Anglers will find more dining and lodging options in Harrisonburg, home to James Madison University (JMU). Here you'll also find two great fly shops, Blue Ridge Angler and Mossy Creek Fly Fishing.

Rating

As far as big trout go, it doesn't get any better than Mossy. When you consider that this creek is completely on private land donated for public use, Mossy Creek handily rates a 10.

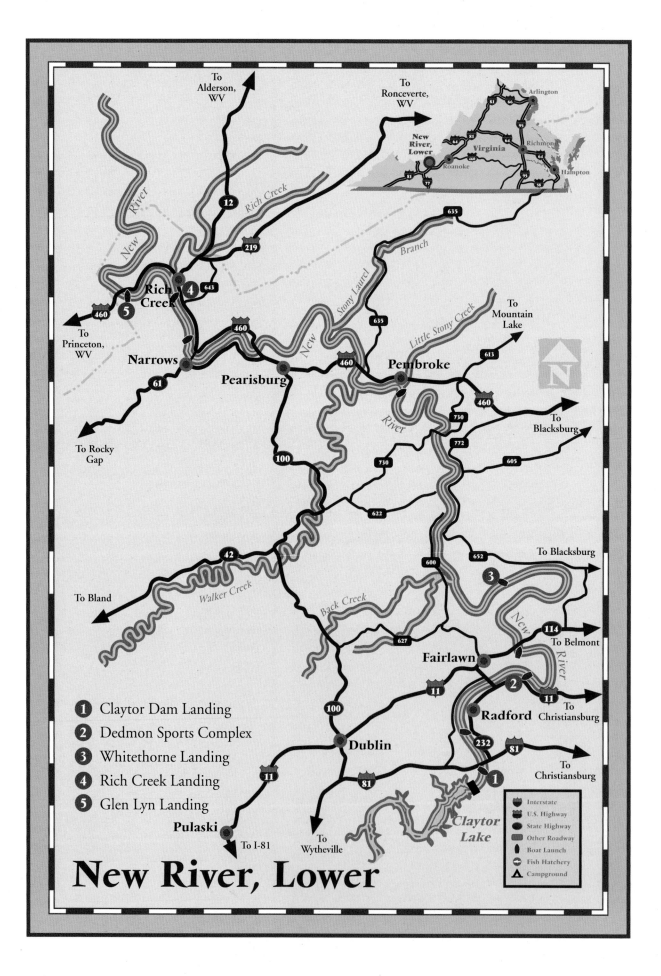

To Alderson, WV

To Ronceverte, WV

New River, Lower

Virginia

Arlington

Richmond

Roanoke

Hampton

12

Rich Creek

219

635

Branch

Stony Laurel

New

Little Stony Creek

To Mountain Lake

Rich Creek

4

643

5

460

To Princeton, WV

460

635

613

Narrows

460

460

Pembroke

460

N

61

Pearisburg

River

730

To Blacksburg

To Rocky Gap

100

730

772

605

622

42

600

652

To Blacksburg

To Bland

Walker Creek

Back Creek

3

New

River

627

114

To Belmont

Fairlawn

2

11

11

To Christiansburg

① Claytor Dam Landing

11

Radford

② Dedmon Sports Complex

232

81

To Christiansburg

③ Whitethorne Landing

100

1

④ Rich Creek Landing

Dublin

⑤ Glen Lyn Landing

81

Claytor Lake

Pulaski

To I-81

To Wytheville

New River, Lower

Interstate
U.S. Highway
State Highway
Other Roadway
Boat Launch
Fish Hatchery
Campground

New River
Lower Section

The lower section of the New River runs for 80 miles from the top of Claytor Lake all the way to the West Virginia state line. You can clearly see the dam at Claytor Lake from Interstate 81, and although dams are not generally thought of as friends to fishing, this dam has helped to prevent flooding and does generate electricity. Built in 1939 by the American Electric Power Company, the dam created Claytor Lake, which stretches out for nearly 4,500 acres, and has provided good habitat for the fish that call this lake home. Once the New River escapes from Claytor Lake, it begins its mad rush north into West Virginia.

The New undergoes a dramatic personality change once it leaves the confines of Claytor Lake: the lower New is much faster than the upper, with class II and III rapids dotting the lower sections of the river. Anglers can look forward to not only great scenery but scores of hungry smallmouth eager to eat their flies. I can tell you from firsthand experience that anglers who do not quickly control their hooked fish may find said fish using the river's strong current against them. I lost a savvy, sizeable smallie

The lower New has a good population of smallmouth bass. Photo by Beau Beasley.

Muskie like this can be found on the lower section of the New River. Always use wire leader when fishing for these brutes. Photo courtesy of Eastern Trophies Fly Fishing.

The lower New has a healthy population of hungry smallmouth bass.
Photo by Lefty Kreh.

here once that got behind me as I was drifting downstream. His ability to use the current against me not only caused me to go quickly into my backing but nearly cost me my fly line.

Blane Chocklett, owner of Blue Ridge Fly Fishers in Roanoke, knows the lower New like the back of his hand and has guided here for well over a decade. Chocklett is also a master fly tyer. Many of his patterns, including the Gummy Minnow and Chocklett's Disc Slider, were developed for use on the New and are particularly effective here—though I've used them elsewhere with enormous success (I recommend them for use on several waters throughout this book). Chocklett is also a pioneer driftboater on the New. That said, wading anglers have much greater access on the lower New than the upper portions, and often anglers will beach their craft and prospect along likely-looking shorelines.

I should mention one additional adjustment that anglers need to allow for when fishing the lower section of the New River, and it has to do with carefully timing your strikes. Unlike other rivers in the state, the lower New stays very clear, and sight fishing for big smallies is common. It's tricky to have the patience to watch a five-pound smallie—or even larger fish like a muskie—rush your fly without striking a bit too soon, which will move the fly away from the fish's mouth. It often takes half a day before even seasoned veterans can get the feel of knowing when to set the hook. I don't exaggerate when I say that 20-inch smallies are common here. The trick, however, is landing them.

The author prefers to use local patterns, including Walt's Popper (left), C.K. Baitfish (center), and Kreelex (right). The fly embroidered on the hat is a Hickey's Condor. Photo by Beau Beasley.

Types of Fish

Smallmouth bass are the predominant species on the lower New River. However a strong population of rock bass exists as well. You may also find muskie by casting many times into deep water. You can catch walleye on the lower section of the New, but they are not nearly as prevalent here as they are on the upper section.

Known Hatches

Crayfish, crickets, damselflies, dragonflies, frogs, hellgrammites, and hoppers, as well as other various baitfish and minnows. Don't be surprised if some hatches go totally ignored here. New River fish are looking for a real meal, and a #18 cricket will most likely not garner much attention.

Equipment to Use

Rods: 7-8 weight, 9-9½ feet in length.
Reels: Standard mechanical. Anglers may get a chance to see their backing if they hook the right fish.
Lines: Weight-forward floating, matched to rod; sink tips can be useful.
Leaders: 1X-2X leaders, 7½-9 feet in length.
Wading: You'll find wading in the lower New River much easier than the upper section, though hiring a guide for your first time is probably a good idea.

Flies to Use

BH Goldilox #4-8, Claw-Dad #2-6, Dover's Peach Fly #6-10, Chocklett's Disc Slider #1/0, Chocklett's Gummy Minnow #6, CK Baitfish #1, Clouser Minnow #1/0-6, Cramer's Jail Bait Minnow #2-4, Finn's Golden Retriever #6-10, Hansen's Electric Frog #6, Hickey's Condor #6-12, Kreelex #2-6, MC2 Crayfish #4-6, San Antonio Worm #4, Shenk's White Minnow #4-6, Walt's Popper #2-12. Many New River anglers throw tandem rigs: for example, a CK Baitfish followed by a Chocklett's Gummy Minnow is a killer combination.

When to Fish

The lower New River fishes well from late April all the way through mid-October in mild seasons. March can also be productive, but you must fish deep and slow.

Season & Limits

New River anglers regularly land smallmouth bass that exceed 16 inches. To get a citation smallmouth in Virginia, however, the fish must exceed five pounds or 20 inches. Check the local game laws for specifics on each species, as they will vary.

Nearby Fly Fishing

Claytor Lake and the upper section of the New are the most obvious alternative choice. You can also trout fish with a small drive to Whitetop Laurel Creek.

Accommodations & Services

Radford is the closet large population base to the lower section of the New River. The closest fly shops are Greasy Creek Outfitters in Floyd County, and Blue Ridge Fly Fishers and the Orvis Company Store, both in Roanoke.

Rating

The lower New River is a must-do fishery. If you are limited to only a few trips a year, this would be a good choice. The lower New River rates an easy 9.

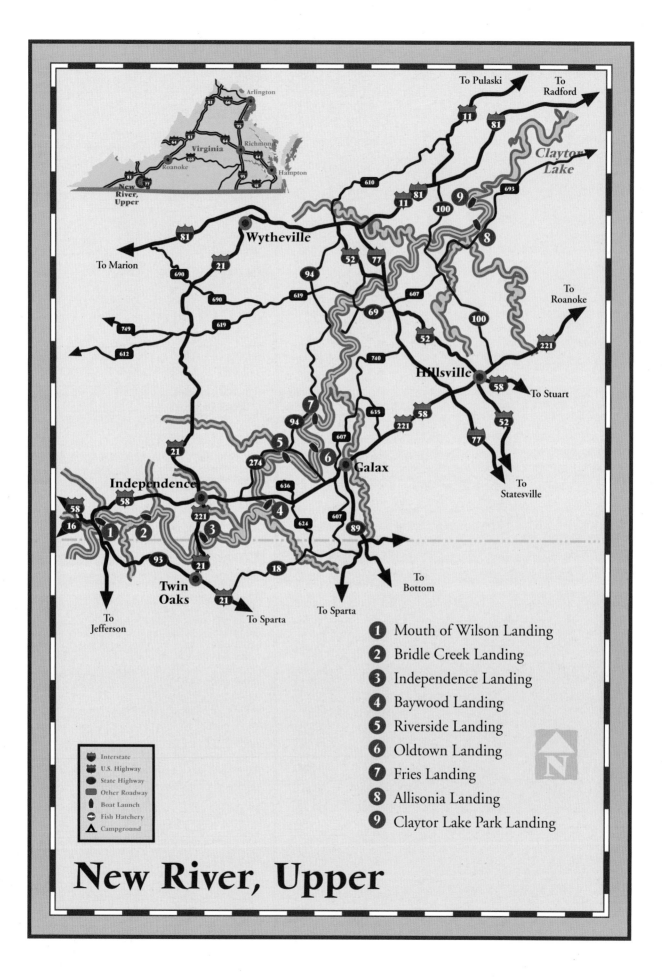

To Pulaski
To Radford

Clayton Lake

Arlington
Virginia
Richmond
Roanoke
Hampton
New River, Upper

Wytheville

To Marion

To Roanoke

To Stuart

Hillsville

Galax

Independence

To Statesville

Twin Oaks

To Jefferson

To Sparta

To Sparta

To Bottom

1 Mouth of Wilson Landing

2 Bridle Creek Landing

3 Independence Landing

4 Baywood Landing

5 Riverside Landing

6 Oldtown Landing

7 Fries Landing

8 Allisonia Landing

9 Claytor Lake Park Landing

Interstate
U.S. Highway
State Highway
Other Roadway
Boat Launch
Fish Hatchery
Campground

N

New River, Upper

New River
Upper Section

In his book *Follow the River*, James Alexander Thom relates the incredible true story of Mary Draper Ingles who, in the summer of 1775 at the age of 23 and eight months pregnant with her third child, was kidnapped by a Shawnee raiding party while her husband was out working in a remote part of their farm near what is now Virginia Tech. Ingles, along with her two young sons and a few other captives, was forcibly marched to a French and Indian village in what is now Ohio. Ingles later fled from her captors when she was taken into West Virginia on a salt-gathering expedition. Under cover of darkness this incredible woman slipped into the night and began the long walk home.

Ingles traveled for 43 days and covered nearly 1,000 miles in rough country with nothing but the clothes on her back, surviving on berries and roots she dug from the ground by hand. When she finally arrived home her husband and remaining neighbors were barely able to recognize her. Not only was she just skin and bones, but her hair had turned completely white at the age of 24. When asked how she had managed to find her way home, she said simply, "I followed the river"—Virginia's New River, that is. Ingles never knew what became of the infant

Brian Coppedge is seen here testing a pontoon boat on New River. Photo by Beau Beasley.

Large rafts like this one allow fly anglers to easily cover miles of river in a day. Photo by Beau Beasley.

Mike Smith of Greasy Creek Outfitters with a nice smallie caught on the New River. Catching 3–5 fish a day like this when the weather is just right is very doable. Photo by Beau Beasley.

she had delivered in captivity. Her youngest son died while living with the Shawnee, but her older son Thomas was returned to the family after 13 years. Ingles went on to have more children and lived to be 83 years old.

We may mentally divide the New River into an upper and lower section—and because the river flows north, the upper section is south of the lower section—with the midpoint being Claytor Lake. The upper New begins just four miles from the Virginia-North Carolina border and zigzags north for more than 150 miles before it enters West Virginia. One unique characteristic of the upper New is that it lacks shore access, due primarily to the river's remoteness and the fact that much of it is surrounded by private land. As a result, fly anglers can expect to enjoy limited pressure on the upper New.

I've had the pleasure of fishing this portion of the New River with Mike Smith, a real pro and owner of Greasy Creek Outfitters. Smith, who is as comfortable on the New as most of us are in our living rooms, is the author of *Fishing the New River Valley: An Angler's Guide* and several other books. "Most guys make the mistake of fishing the New River like some of the smaller warm water rivers in this state. They show up with these little 3- to 4-inch dinky flies, and I just tell them to save those for when they're trout fishing," Smith says with a chuckle. "When you come to fish on the New, you need to think big fish." Sound like bragging to you? Well, keep in mind that Smith's clients routinely land more than three-pound smallmouth and in 2003 one of his clients landed a 13-pound, 9-ounce walleye. Smith has fished here for 30 years, floated the upper New River thousands of times, and believes that it remains one of the most pristine places in Virginia. Having fished the New on a number of occasions, I'm inclined to agree. The scenery is impressive—and so are the lunker smallies.

Smallmouth bass often fall hard for well placed poppers.
Photo by Beau Beasley.

Types of Fish

Most anglers floating the New pursue smallies, but trophy walleye, white bass, and black crappie might also be on the menu. Resident upper New River muskie are normally caught on spinning gear. However, guides like Mike Smith and Blane Chocklett do target these fish at times with fly anglers. Also, it is not uncommon to catch stripers here.

Known Hatches

Ants, beetles, crayfish, crickets, damselflies, dragonflies, frogs, hellgrammites, and hoppers call the New River home. Don't miss the large spring migration of shad fry coming out of Claytor Lake, a major source of food for the larger fish in the New.

Equipment to Use

Rods: 7-8 weight, 9-9½ feet in length.
Reels: Standard mechanical, although you may see your backing if you hook the right fish.
Lines: Weight-forward floating, matched to rod. Sink tips can be useful.
Leaders: 1X-2X leaders, 7½-9 feet in length.
Wading: The upper New River is best floated with a guide.

Flies to Use

Claw-Dad #2-6, Chocklett's Disc Slider #1/0, Chocklett's Gummy Minnow #6, CK Baitfish #1, Clouser Minnow #1/0-2, Cramer's Jail Bait Minnow #2-4, Hansen's Electric Frog #6, Kreelex #2, MC2 Crayfish #4, San Antonio Worm #4, Shenk's White Minnow #4, Trow's Minnow #1/0-4, Walt's Popper #2. Keep the shad fry population in mind and be prepared to toss streamers and big poppers for these larger fish.

When to Fish

Although you can fish the New River all year, the best times are April through the early part of October. Sometimes fly anglers may have to wait until May before action really heats up because the river is deep and warming it sufficiently takes time, particularly in the upper section.

Season & Limits

The New is open all year for fishing. Limits on sizes and amounts of fish will vary according to species.

Nearby Fly Fishing

The lower New is the most obvious alternative choice. You can also fish Claytor Lake and, if you don't mind a small drive, Whitetop Laurel Creek.

Accommodations & Services

Galax is the closest sizable city to the mouth of the New River, but Radford is also an option for dining and lodging. Be sure to visit Shot Tower State Park and Foster Fall Park as well, where you will find a beautiful hiking trail that flanks the river for nearly 50 miles (though you'll find limited access to the actual water along the trail).

Rating

The upper New is a wonderful river with a rich history. Unfortunately it does not lend itself to wading because limited public access is available. Your best bet is to hire a guide or canoe or kayak the river yourself. The upper portion of the New River rates a 9.

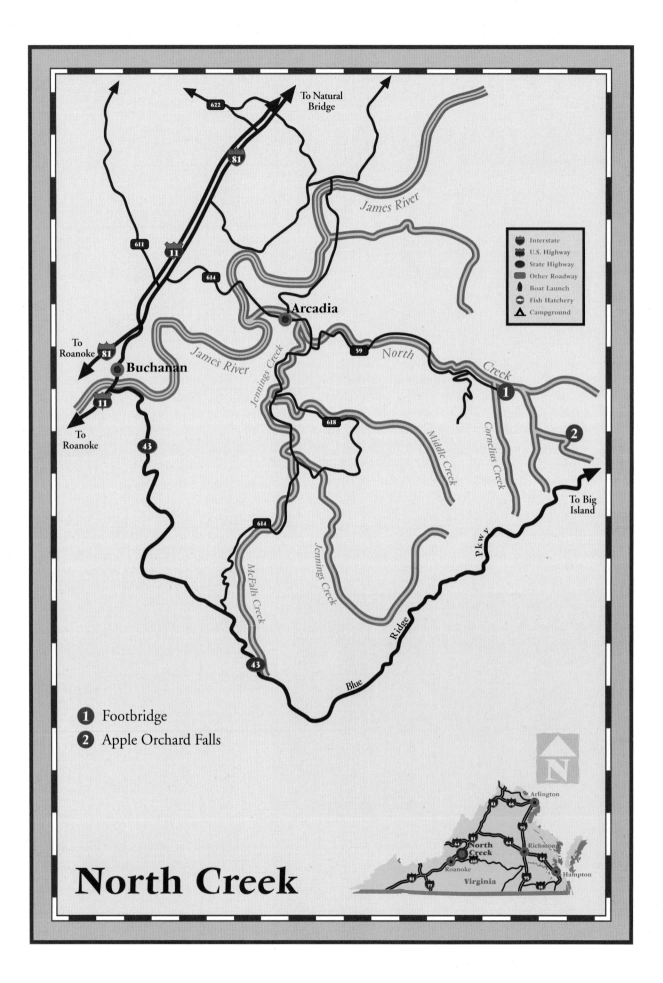

1 Footbridge

2 Apple Orchard Falls

North Creek

North Creek

Situated in scenic Botetourt County near Natural Bridge, the North Creek deserves any serious trout angler's attention. Although there is good water throughout North Creek, it's the catch-and-release trout portion in the uppermost section above the campgrounds of North Creek that garners most fly anglers' attention. North Creek is crisscrossed several times by Rt. 59, which allows for easy access. I recommend driving to the end of Rt. 59 and beginning to fish after crossing over the wooden bridge near the information kiosk. Cornelius Creek, a small feeder stream, enters North Creek just past the wooden bridge. If North Creek is too high, you could try this small stream as an alternative.

North Creek has a good hiking trail that stays within sight of the creek at almost every point and also has quite a few bridges—built for hikers—that cross the stream. The high canopy cover along the stream gives it almost a rainforest look and provides a great deal of shade for anglers. Thick green ferns finish off this landscape, giving the whole area a fairy-tale look. Good pools are formed by lichen-covered rocks and large trees, some of which have diameters that exceed 18 inches and which provide great cover for the local trout.

Two other aspects of the area make North Creek particularly attractive to outdoor lovers. For some reason this area attracts South American birds that use this part of the forest as a layover point during their migration. Another interesting sight is Apple Orchard Falls, a 200-foot waterfall that lies two miles from the first bridge you come to at the end of Rt. 59. This is not your traditional waterfall, cascading down uninterrupted. In fact, Apple Orchard Falls stair-steps down over several rock ledges and is clogged at points with fallen trees. The hike leading to the falls is clearly laid out, and the Forest Service does an excellent job of keeping the trails clear. Natural rocks have been used as stepping stones to give hikers and anglers easier footing, and these steps have been laid with a precision that would make a stonemason proud.

One of the three footbridges that cross North Creek. Thick forestation means that terrestrial patterns are a good choice here. Photo by Beau Beasley.

Types of Fish
The lower end of North Creek contains stocked rainbows; the upper section has wild brook trout as well as wild rainbows.

Known Hatches
Winter Stoneflies, Blue Quills, Blue Wing Olives, Hendricksons, March Browns, Little Yellow Stoneflies, Sulfurs, Quill Gordons, Caddis, Cahills, inchworms, and other terrestrials.

Equipment to Use
Rods: 2-4 weight, 7-8 feet in length.
Reels: Mechanical and palm.
Lines: Weight-forward floating, matched to rod.
Leaders: 4X-6X, 9 feet in length.
Wading: Hip waders are fine here.

Flies to Use
Dries: Adams #14-20, BWO #14-20, Braided Butt Damsel #10-12, Dusty's Deviant #12-16, Elk Hair Caddis #14-20, Flying Ant #10-18, Gelso's Little Black Stonefly #16-20, Lt. Cahill #14-20, Little Yellow Sally #14-20, March Brown #10-14, Murray's Mr. Rapidan #14-20, Pale Morning Dun #14-20, Quill Gordon #12-22, Stimulator #12-20, Steeves' Attract Ant #16-20, Steeves' Bark Beetle #16-20, Steeves' Crystal Butt Cricket #8-10, Steeves' Disc O' Beetle #14, Steeves' UFO #10.
Nymphs & Streamers: Beadhead Goldilox #6-10, Beadhead Hare's Ear #14-20, Beadhead Prince Nymph #14-20, Bruce's Little Bow #6, Coburn's Cress Bug #14-20, Coburn's Inchworm #12-14, Egg #6-20, Finn's Golden Retriever #6-10, Green Weenie #14-16, Matuka #4-10, Mickey Finn #6-10, MC2 Crayfish #4-6, Muddler Minnow #6-10, Murray's Marauder #6-10, Pheasant Tail #14-20, River Witch #6, Scud #10-18, Sculpin #4-8, Woolly Bugger #6-10.

When to Fish
North Creek fishes well from late March through November. Keep in mind, however, that water levels can be quite low in the summer—have a backup plan for other options.

Season & Limits
The lower portion of North Creek is a put-and-take fishery. The upper reaches of North Creek beyond the campground just off Route 59 is special-regulation, catch-and-release fishing only.

Nearby Fly Fishing
Close alternatives include the Maury River and the Shenandoah National Park.

Accommodations & Services
The small town of Buchanan is the largest population center near North Creek, though you may have to travel as far as Natural Bridge to find a hotel. There are no nearby fly shops, so go prepared.

Rating
North Creek is a medium-sized stream that can keep you busy all day. Although these are small fish, the catch-and-release-only section is a real plus for fly anglers—and for this reason, I rate North Creek a 7.

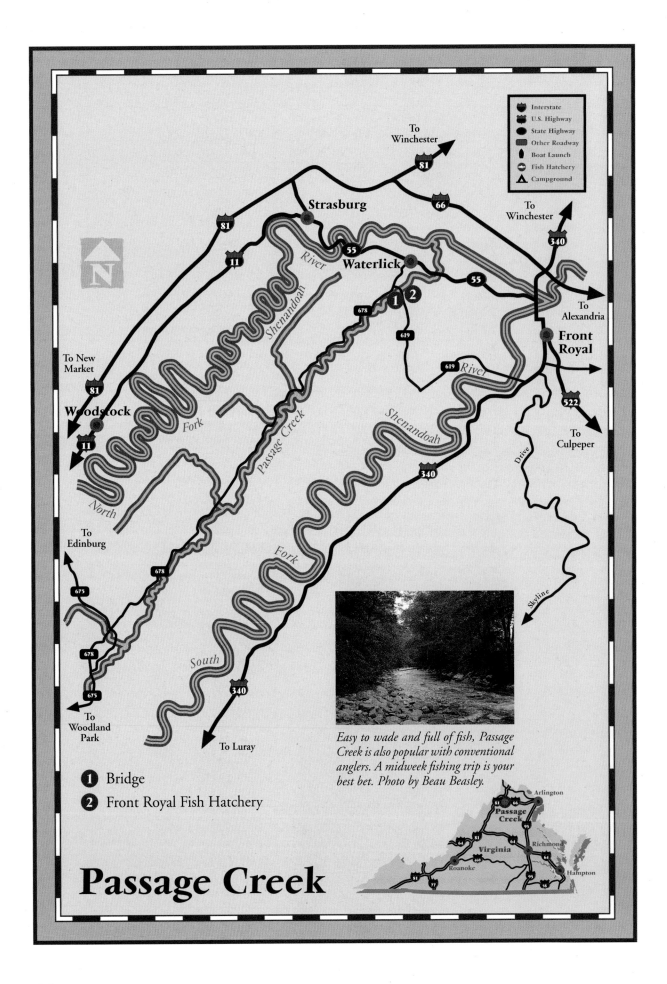

To Winchester

Strasburg

Waterlick

To Winchester

To Alexandria

Front Royal

To New Market

To Culpeper

Woodstock

To Edinburg

River

Shenandoah

Fork

Passage Creek

Shenandoah

River

Drive

Skyline

North

Fork

South

To Woodland Park

To Luray

Interstate
U.S. Highway
State Highway
Other Roadway
Boat Launch
Fish Hatchery
Campground

N

① Bridge

② Front Royal Fish Hatchery

Easy to wade and full of fish, Passage Creek is also popular with conventional anglers. A midweek fishing trip is your best bet. Photo by Beau Beasley.

Passage Creek

Arlington
Passage Creek
Virginia
Richmond
Roanoke
Hampton

Passage Creek

From its upper portion southwest of Front Royal, through private farmland and the George Washington National Forest, to its runs between the north and south forks of the Shenandoah River, beautiful Passage Creek is a larger body of water than its name implies. Its runs and riffles occasionally stretch around the cliff-like shale walls of Massanutten Mountain to the east and Green Mountain to the west. This is pretty country, and the mountain laurel that blooms along the banks of Passage Creek adds much ambience to any fishing experience.

One of the main reference points for this water, and a good access point as well, is the Mountain Road bridge (Route 619). This bridge marks the beginning of the special regulation, fly-fishing-only section of water just a stone's throw from the state fish hatchery, a large stone building surrounded by several retaining ponds. Though the pulse may quicken at the idea of fishing near a hatchery, alas—this outfit raises walleye and not trout. Occasionally trout are brought here to rest before they are sent to other stocking locations.

Limited parking exists next to the bridge itself. The deep water beneath the bridge looks inviting, as do the surrounding exposed tree roots along the banks, but make no mistake: this water gets fished hard. Instead, move 100 yards above or below the bridge before attempting to cast. Below the bridge the stream narrows, and anglers will find large pools and runs twisting around high embankments loaded with brush. Above the bridge anglers will find good water as well, with plenty of deadfall from nearby trees that have been toppled as a result of erosion. A good hike above the bridge reveals what looks like a small waterfall created by a low-level dam. This is actually a concrete structure designed to divert water into the hatchery retaining ponds when needed.

Anglers can also access Passage Creek at several places off of Route 678, which runs along the creek's banks above the hatchery. You will need a trout stamp in addition to your fishing license to fish in the special regulation section and also a stamp if fishing in the George Washington National Forest. The special regulation section extends from the lower boundary of the Front Royal Fish Hatchery, upstream 0.9 miles to the Shenandoah/Warren County line.

Types of Fish
Rainbow trout, brown trout, bluegill, and the occasional smallmouth bass and sucker fish.

Known Hatches
Winter Stonefly, Hendrickson, March Brown, Little Yellow Stonefly, Sulfur, Caddis, Cahill, inchworm, terrestrials, and Slate Drake.

Equipment to Use
Rods: 4-6 weight, 7-8½ feet in length.
Reels: Standard mechanical or palm.
Lines: Weight forward floating lines matched to rod.
Leaders: 4X to 6X, 9 feet in length.
Wading: You can get by with hip boots, but chest waders can be useful here.

Flies to Use
Dries: Adams #14-20, BWO #14-20, Braided Butt Damsel #10-12, Dusty's Deviant #12-16, Elk Hair Caddis #14-20, Flying Ant #10-18, Gelso's Little Black Stonefly #16-20, Lt. Cahill #14-20, Little Yellow Sally #14-20, March Brown #10-14, Murray's Mr. Rapidan #14-20, Pale Morning Dun #14-20, Quill Gordon #12-22, Stimulator #12-20, Steeves' Attract Ant #16-20, Steeves' Bark Beetle #16-20, Steeves' Crystal Butt Cricket #8-10, Steeves' Disc O' Beetle #14, Steeves' UFO #10.
Nymphs & Streamers: BH Goldilox #6-10, BH Hare's Ear #14-20, BH Prince Nymph #14-20, Bruce's Little Bow #6, Coburn's Cress Bug #14-20, Coburn's Inchworm #12-14, Egg #6-20, Finn's Golden Retriever #6-10, Green Weenie #14-16, Matuka #4-10, Mickey Finn #6-10, MC2 Crayfish #4-6, Muddler Minnow #6-10, Murray's Marauder #6-10, Pheasant Tail #14-20, River Witch #6, Scud #10-18, Sculpin #4-8, Woolly Bugger #6-10.

When to Fish
Open all year.

Season & Limits
From October through the following May, anglers may use only artificial lures and must return all fish. From June through September, general trout regulations are in effect.

Nearby Fly Fishing
If Passage Creek is crowded, try one of the other trout streams in the Shenandoah National Park. Or go after warm water species in either fork of the Shenandoah River.

Accommodations & Services
Front Royal, just off Route 340, boasts a number of lodging options.

Rating
Passage Creek is a solid 7.

Downed trees are great structure for trout. The fish that strikes your fly will want to run under the tree so play your fish accordingly.
Photo by Beau Beasley.

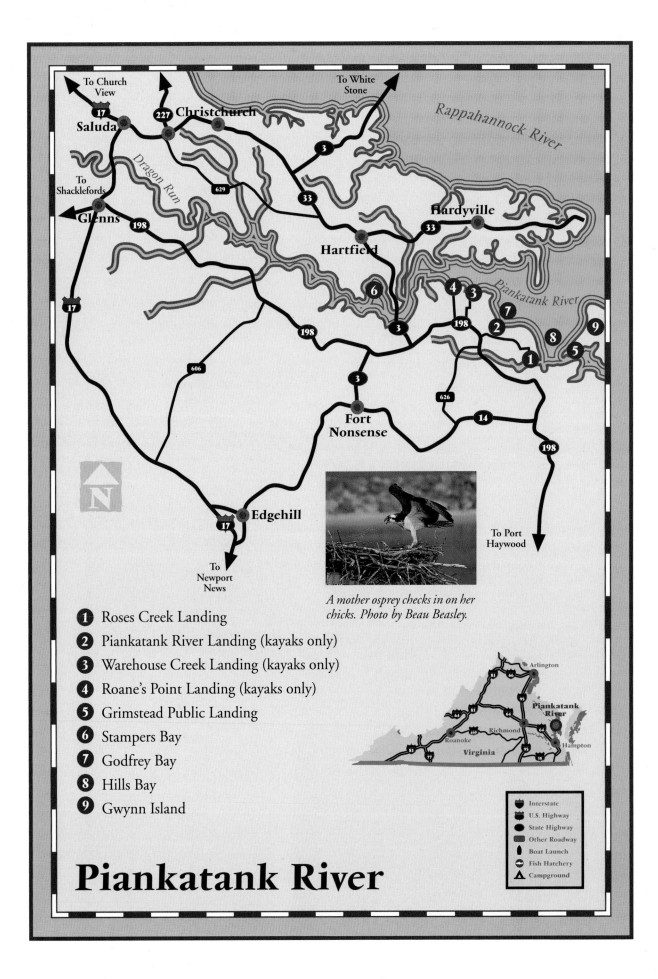

To Church View
To White Stone
17 Saluda
227 Christchurch
3
Dragon Run
629
To Shacklefords
33
Hardyville
Glenns
198
33
Piankatank River
Hartfield
17
6
4
3
198
7
9
198
2
8
1
5
606
626
3
14
Fort Nonsense
198
To Port Haywood
N
17 Edgehill
To Newport News

A mother osprey checks in on her chicks. Photo by Beau Beasley.

1 Roses Creek Landing

2 Piankatank River Landing (kayaks only)

3 Warehouse Creek Landing (kayaks only)

4 Roane's Point Landing (kayaks only)

5 Grimstead Public Landing

6 Stampers Bay

7 Godfrey Bay

8 Hills Bay

9 Gwynn Island

Arlington
Piankatank River
Richmond
Roanoke
Hampton
Virginia

Interstate
U.S. Highway
State Highway
Other Roadway
Boat Launch
Fish Hatchery
Campground

Piankatank River

Piankatank River

Named for the Native American tribe that Captain John Smith documented living on her shores in 1608, the Piankatank is perhaps one of the best-kept saltwater secrets in the Old Dominion. I chose to cover the Piankatank River for this book precisely because I don't remember ever reading anything about it—though the river has a reputation as a prime fishing location among spin fishermen. Sandwiched between Mathews and Middlesex Counties, the Piankatank is easily accessed off Route 17 and is a mere 90-minute drive from Richmond.

The Piankatank River is the home waters of Captain Chris Newsome, who is a native of Mathews County. He's fished the creeks and areas surrounding these waters his entire life. Captain Newsome believes that the Piankatank may well be one of the most pristine rivers in the state as a result of the lack of industrial development on its shores. The closest things you'll find to development are the stately homes that dot the landscape around the river's edge and the occasional hunter's duck blind.

The Piankatank River is easy on fly anglers because much of the river is protected from the wind by the shoreline that at times is merely a few hundred yards apart. Those who'd like to launch their own boats will find plenty of access; it's a wonderful area to explore with a kayak as well. Anglers can expect to find plenty to catch during the spring and fall runs of migrating fish. A good resident population of fish exists as well. Boat docks, oyster reefs, and the occasional island along the banks of the Piankatank River ensure that you'll have plenty of structure to fish around.

Ideally situated between swampy Dragon Run and the Chesapeake Bay, the Piankatank River holds plenty of promise for those willing to work for it. Although it can be a challenge, anglers can catch stripers in the bottom of the river near the Bay and try for bass in the top of the river near Dragon Run in the same day.

Dead trees provide excellent structure for fish. Photo by Beau Beasley.

Types of Fish

You can never be sure what you're going to pull out of the Piankatank, though stripers and blues are a safe bet. You will also find a healthy population of flounder and speckled trout as well as croaker. Don't be too surprised, however, if you begin pulling largemouth bass out of the upper regions of the river.

Known Baitfish

Anglers fishing in and around the Piankatank River can expect to see menhaden, shrimp, squid, crabs, a variety of small baitfish, and eels.

Equipment to Use

Rods: 6-9 weight, 8 to 9½ feet in length.
Reels: Standard mechanical unless you get into larger fish—in which case you will need a good drag.
Lines: Weight-forward floating lines and fast-intermediate sinking lines matched to rod.
Leaders: 1X-3X, 9 feet in length.
Wading: You will need a boat to fish this river effectively.

Flies to Use

Bruce's Bay Anchovy #2, Bruce's Crystal Shrimp #1/0, Clouser Minnow #2/0-4, DuBiel's Finesse Fly #2-4, DuBiel's Lil'haden #1/0-2, DuBiel's Red-Ducer #1/0-2, Lefty's Deceiver #2/0-2, Lefty's Half and Half, #2/0-2, Russell's Mussel #1/0-1, Tommy's Crease Fly #2/0-2, Tommy's Eel Fly #2/0-1/0, Trow's Minnow #3/0-6.

When to Fish

The Piankatank holds promise year-round.

Season & Limits

The Piankatank feeds directly into the Chesapeake Bay, so it's no surprise that the river's prime fishing season mirrors that of the Bay. The best time for fly anglers is late March to late November.

Nearby Fly Fishing

Anglers on the Piankatank can easily fish Dragon Run, which feeds the Piankatank, and the Chesapeake Bay.

Accommodations & Services

At the eastern end of Virginia's Middle Peninsula and on the north shore of the Piankatank is Deltaville, a Mid-Atlantic fishing mecca. Anglers will find lodging and dining options that cater specifically to them. By contrast you'll find that Gloucester, the closest town if you are approaching the Piankatank from the south, has fewer such options.

Rating

The Piankatank has much to offer fly anglers. Because it is easily accessible, full of fish, and fairly free of pressure I would rate the Piankatank River an 8.

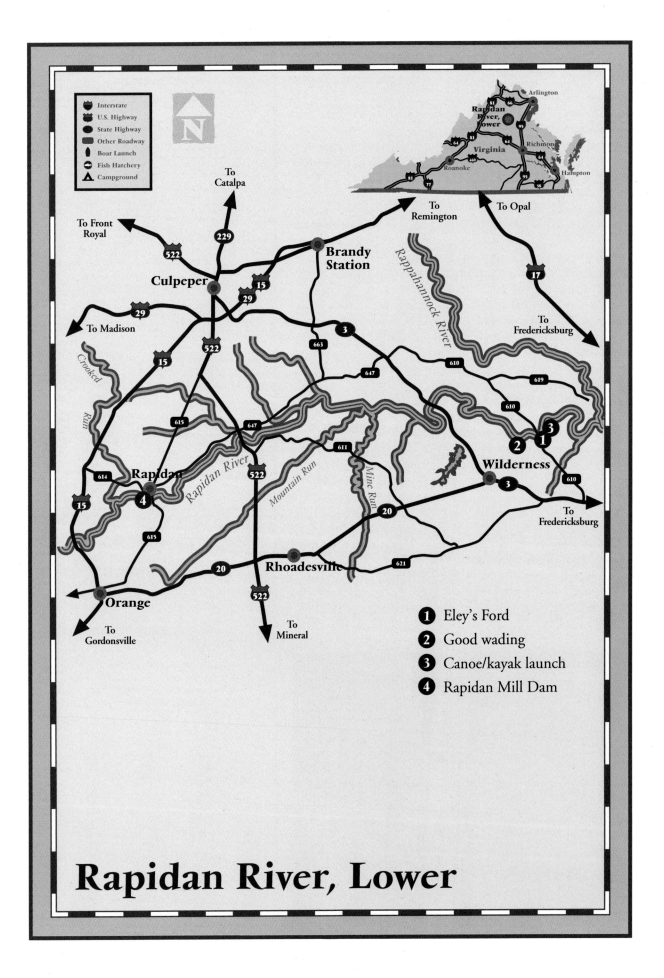

Rapidan River, Lower

Rapidan River
Lower Section

When you say that you're headed out to fish the Rapidan, the vast majority of fly anglers will assume that you're in the market for a glorious day of brook trout fishing. A logical assumption, right? But the really sharp fly angler will ask you if you're going after trout or smallmouth bass. Yes, one of the best-kept secrets in Virginia is the warm water fishing opportunities on the Rapidan. Once the Rapidan leaves the Shenandoah National Park, it begins to gather warmer lowland waters and eventually empties into the Rappahannock River, which in turn empties into the Chesapeake Bay.

One of the easiest access points to the lower Rapidan is in the town of Rapidan itself directly off of route 615. (Perhaps town is a bit of a stretch—a more appropriate word might be village—but call it what you will, it's easy to reach the river from here.) Anglers can park just south of the bridge alongside the now-defunct Rapidan Mills or above the bridge closer to the north side of the river. There are only two spaces available in the northern lot, and no parking is permitted here from dusk to dawn. From this lot a well-worn path leads straight to the river, but be forewarned: this area is very popular with local spin fishermen, so be prepared to move above or below the Rapidan Mills Dam.

Jim Atkinson (left) of the Shenandoah National Park Service and Dan Genest of the Fly Fishers of Virginia discuss fish samples collected on the Rapidan. Photo by Beau Beasley.

Though many fly anglers fish the upper Rapidan, the lower section sees much less pressure. Photo by Beau Beasley.

If you use a canoe or kayak, stop and wade off the islands.
Photo by Beau Beasley.

The old Rapidan Mill and Dam provide a historic backdrop for a day's fishing.
Photo by Beau Beasley.

It also doesn't hurt to scout out the river from the bridge. On my last trip the water was crystal clear, and I had no problem seeing some really nice fish.

Perhaps the best access point for the lower Rapidan is at Eley's Ford off of Route 610. This is also a designated VDGIF canoe launch, so bring along your kayak or canoe if you have one. Plenty of parking is available on the south side of the bridge. Don't be surprised to see another fly angler here, although this area too is quite popular with spin fishermen.

There are small islands that spring up along the lower Rapidan, so don't miss the chance to fish around them when the opportunity presents itself.

Incidentally, it was near Eley's Ford that Confederate General J.E.B. Stuart was informed that General Stonewall Jackson had been gravely wounded and that Stuart would therefore need to assume Jackson's command. The Battle of Chancellorsville was fought just a few miles south of this section of the lower Rapidan. As they crossed the picturesque Rapidan, I imagine that these brave men considered how much more pleasant a day on the river would be with a fly rod in hand instead of a musket.

This serene stretch of river is only a few miles from some of the bloodiest fighting in the Civil War. Photo by Beau Beasley.

Types of Fish

Smallmouth bass rule the roost, but you can also occasionally catch a largemouth bass and of course lots of other sunfish like bluegills. Occasionally catfish and rock bass put in appearances as well. The closer you get to the Rappahannock River, which is fed by the Rapidan, the more likely you are to catch shad in early to mid-April.

Known Hatches

Ants, beetles, crayfish, crickets, damselflies, dragonflies, frogs, hellgrammites, hoppers, and various baitfish and minnows call this river home. I recently observed a U.S. Fish and Wildlife Service sampling of the Rapidan River, and I was surprised at the number of sculpins.

Equipment to Use

Rods: 4-7 weight, 8-9 feet in length.
Reels: Standard mechanical.
Lines: Weight-forward floating, matched to rod; the occasional sink tip may be used.
Leaders: 3X-5X leaders, 9 feet in length.
Wading: You can use hip waders, but chest waders are much better.

Flies to Use

BH Goldilox #4-8, Bruce's Little Bow #2-6, Claw-Dad #2-6, Chocklett's Gummy Minnow #6, CK Baitfish #1, Clouser Minnow #2-6, Cramer's Jail Bait Minnow #2-4, Finn's Golden Retriever #6-10, Hansen's Electric Frog #6, Hickey's Condor #6-12, Kreelex #2-6, MC2 Crayfish #4-6, Murray's Lead Eye Hellgrammite #6, Murray's Marauder #6, Patuxent Special #6-10, San Antonio Worm #4, Shenk's White Minnow #4-6, Super Patuxent Special #6-10, Trow's Minnow #2-6, Walt's Popper #2-12.

When to Fish

May through October is prime time to go after most species in the lower Rapidan. You can, however, catch shad in the lower sections starting in mid-April.

Season & Limits

Check with the local game laws for creel limits.

Nearby Fly Fishing

From here you are also close to the Rappahannock and the waters of the Shenandoah National Park.

Accommodations & Services

Your best bet when fishing the lower Rapidan is to consider charming Culpeper as your base of operations. The town has become a mecca for regional specialty foods. With unique and acclaimed restaurants, lodging options, and The Castaway Company, a full-service fly shop in the heart of downtown, you could hardly do better.

Rating

The lower Rapidan rates a 6—but under the right conditions, it can rate an 8.

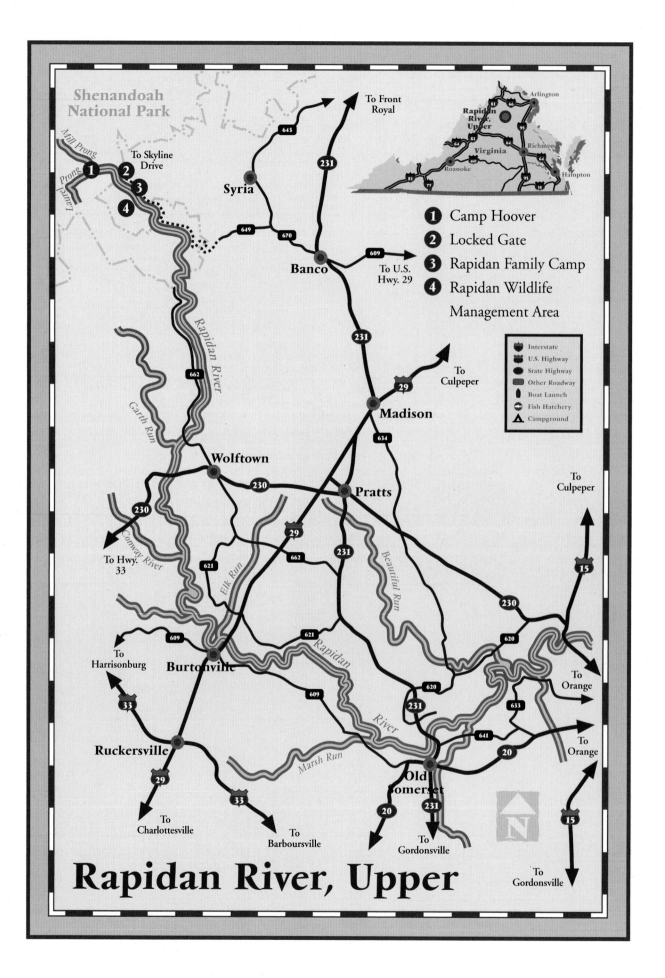

Rapidan River, Upper

Rapidan River
Upper Section

The Rapidan River is the best-known trout stream in the Shenandoah National Park and perhaps, some would argue, in the entire Old Dominion, for two reasons: first, fly anglers know that the Rapidan is the best place in Virginia to catch wild brook trout. Second, President Herbert Hoover loved fly fishing the river so much that he built a camp at its headwaters where he entertained the Prime Minister of Great Britain as well as other international dignitaries. Once while fishing the Rapidan I noticed a large stone fireplace with a chimney standing by itself in the middle of a small clearing. I asked a park employee if one of the cabins had burned down leaving only this majestic stone fireplace in its stead. The employee grinned and informed me that the fireplace had been built to serve as a prop: President Hoover and his fellow luminaries would gather around it at the end of the day. Essentially, this grand stone chimney was merely a setting for photo ops.

In the summer of 2006, the Fly Fishers of Virginia assisted the U.S. Fish and Wildlife Service (USFWS) in stream sampling the Rapidan. I watched as some USFWS employees shocked the water while others netted the resulting stunned fish. They then

President Hoover's "photo op" on the Rapidan: The stone fireplace still stands at Camp Hoover today. Photo by Beau Beasley.

Members of the Fly Fishers of Virginia often assist the U.S. Fish and Wildlife Service with stream sampling on the upper Rapidan. Photo by Beau Beasley.

Rich Hiegel of Richmond, Virginia, fishing a quiet pool on the Rapidan River. Photo by Beau Beasley.

passed the netted fish to volunteers with buckets who carried the fish to a holding area until the biologist on the scene could weigh, measure, and count the specimens. I saw some nice brook trout that day—some measuring up to nine inches long. But I was amazed by other catches, including a huge selection of suckers, crayfish, sculpins, and other minnows, along with a yellow-bellied catfish. And the strangest net of the day? An eel over two and half feet long in one of the larger pools.

Anglers can access the Rapidan from Route 662 near Wolftown. Park at the end of the road and then hike upstream. To fish higher in the park next to Camp Hoover, access the Rapidan from Route 649, Quaker Run Rd. This is a tough and winding road that doubles back on itself in places, and when the hard surface stops, you still have 7.5 miles of rough road before reaching a locked gate. The drive will take you in and out of the SNP as well as the Rapidan Wildlife Management Area before the road ends. Drive carefully as you may pass other vehicles or anglers on the road. Take time to walk upstream or downstream if you see a car parked on the side of the road. Distance makes good fishing pals. To view Camp Hoover, park at the end of Route 649 by the locked gate and then hike up the service road for about a mile. It can be a long walk to Camp Hoover but it's worth it—besides you can always fish on the way up.

Hip boots are perfect for fishing small mountain streams.
Photo by Beau Beasley.

Types of Fish
This is wild brook trout heaven.

Known Hatches
Different fly hatches can occur throughout the day on the Rapidan as with other mountain trout streams. These hatches include but are not limited to Winter Stoneflies, Blue Quills, Blue Wing Olives, Hendricksons, March Browns, Little Yellow Stoneflies, Sulfurs, Quill Gordons, Caddis, Cahills, inchworms, and terrestrials. This fast-flowing stream forces the trout to make quick decisions as to what to eat, so at times they'll hit almost anything. At other times you'd swear the river is fishless. The trick is finding out what they want and then delivering it—sometimes in tight quarters as a result of nearby shoreline trees and shrubs.

Equipment to Use
Rods: 3-4 weight, 6½-8 feet in length.
Reels: Standard mechanical.
Lines: Weight-forward floating, matched to rod.
Leaders: 4X-7X leaders, 9 feet in length.
Wading: Hip waders are fine here.

Flies to Use
Dries: Adams #14-20, BWO #14-20, Braided Butt Damsel #10-12, Dusty's Deviant #12-16, Elk Hair Caddis #14-20, Flying Ant #10-18, Gelso's Little Black Stonefly #16-20, Lt. Cahill #14-20, Little Yellow Sally #14-20, March Brown #10-14, Murray's Mr. Rapidan #14-20, Pale Morning Dun #14-20, Quill Gordon #12-22, Stimulator #12-20, Steeves' Attract Ant #16-20, Steeves' Bark Beetle #16-20, Steeves' Crystal Butt Cricket #8-10, Steeves' Disc O' Beetle #14, Steeves' UFO #10.
Nymphs & Streamers: Beadhead Goldilox #6-10, Beadhead Hare's Ear #14-20, Beadhead Prince Nymph #14-20, Bruce's Little Bow #6, Coburn's Cress Bug #14-20, Coburn's Inchworm #12-14, Egg #6-20, Finn's Golden Retriever #6-10, Green Weenie #14-16, Matuka #4-10, Mickey Finn #6-10, MC2 Crayfish #4-6, Muddler Minnow #6-10, Murray's Marauder #6-10, Pheasant Tail #14-20, River Witch #6, Scud #10-18, Sculpin #4-8, Woolly Bugger #6-10.

When to Fish
Fishing is best on the upper Rapidan in the early spring and right through the fall. Even after a hard rain, this stream tends to clear very quickly due to its solid rock bottom.

Season & Limits
You can fish the Rapidan year-round, but I feel strongly that you should never remove a trout from this water.

Nearby Fly Fishing
Numerous Shenandoah National Park streams are an easy drive from the upper Rapidan.

Accommodations & Services
Sperryville is the nearest place for food and gas, but if you hope to spend the night consider nearby Luray. The Luray Caverns can be a real delight for the non-anglers in your life. The closest fly shops are Rhodes Fly Shop in Warrenton and The Castaway Company in Culpeper.

Rating
The Rapidan is a must-do mountain trout stream that rates a 9.

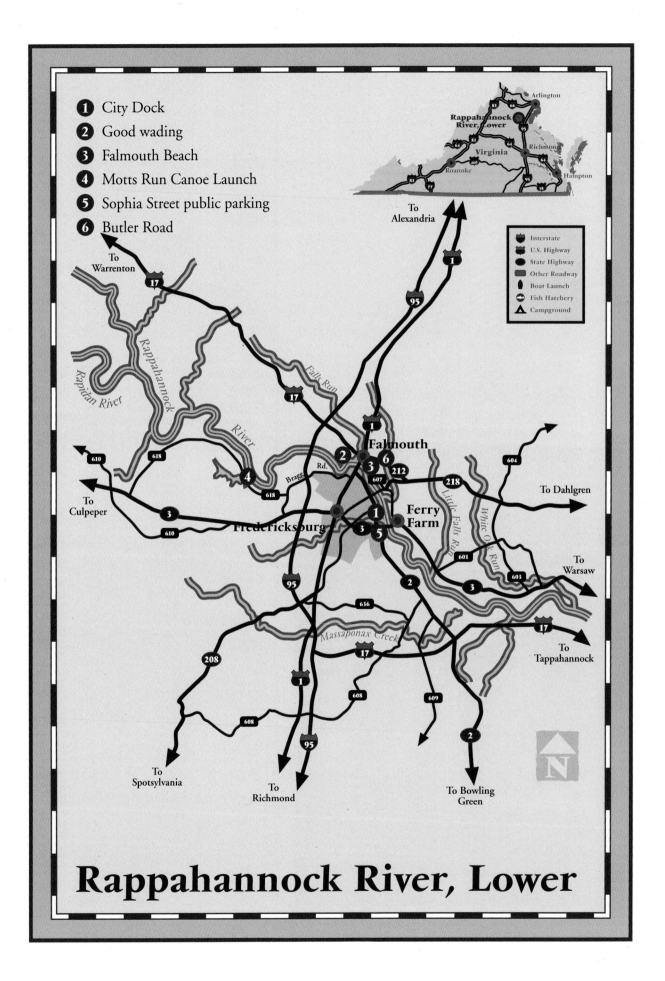

1 City Dock
2 Good wading
3 Falmouth Beach
4 Motts Run Canoe Launch
5 Sophia Street public parking
6 Butler Road

Rappahannock River, Lower

Rappahannock River
Lower Section

Strong fighters, shad surge upstream in the spring by the thousands. Release your catch as quickly as possible. Photo by King Montgomery.

Virginia's Rappahannock, affectionately known as the Rap, has a long and colorful history. Algonquian Indians named the river Rappahannock, meaning "rapidly rising and falling waters," no doubt referring to its daily tidal fluctuations as it empties into Chesapeake Bay. Legend has it that George Washington was alongside the Rappahannock riverbank when he cut down that famous cherry tree with his trusty ax and later came clean about the dirty deed. Indeed, the first president grew up on his sister's plantation Ferry Farm nearby and no doubt fished the Rap as a youth. Virginia's spectacular cherry trees bloom at precisely the same time of the year that the shad migrate up the Rappahannock. I like to think that George was merely fashioning his own fly rod.

From its humble beginnings in the Blue Ridge Mountains, past the famed Rapidan River and then to its final destination at the sea, the Rappahannock includes many miles of float- and wade-friendly fishable water. From the last week in March through the first week in May, fly anglers flock to the Rap in search of hard-fighting shad. These scrappy fish, which migrate upriver by the tens of thousands from the Chesapeake Bay, may have lived as long as five years at sea before returning to the river to spawn. Urging the shad along to their own spawning grounds are striped bass, which feed heavily on the shad as they migrate upstream. And if anglers don't consider shad or stripers worthy opponents, the river boasts a healthy and active resident population of perch, bluegill, gar, and large and smallmouth bass.

Fly angler Paul Kearney into a nice fish on the lower Rap. Photo by King Montgomery.

A view of the lower Rappahannock from the Route 1 bridge.
Photo by Beau Beasley.

Careful where you wade: sandbars shift often on the lower Rap
as a result of flooding. Photo by Beau Beasley.

Spin fishermen favor the Rap during shad season and fly anglers should expect to share water with paddlers, kayakers, and canoers. Fredericksburg owns a great deal of land adjacent to the riverbank, which families frequent throughout the summer.

The best access is off River Road near Falmouth Waterfront Park. The area is managed by Fredericksburg-Stafford Park Authority, and you'll need a parking permit which runs $2.50 for all year from their office at 60 Butler Rd. in Falmouth. Anglers can fish the river when the park is closed to other activities. For updates call the park office at 540-373-7909. There is free parking at Sophia St. on the other side of the Route 3 bridge. This parking lot sits alongside the river, so if the fish aren't biting you can walk around Old Town Fredericksburg and enjoy one of the country's most important historical cities.

In 2003 the Army Corps of Engineers brought down the Embry Dam, long the bane of the shad's existence, adding over 100 miles of additional spawning grounds for native fish. The removal of the dam also makes traversing the river easier for kayakers and anglers alike. Conservation groups like the Friends of the Rappahannock and the Falmouth Fly Fishers Club worked hard to take down the dam, and anglers and river enthusiasts owe them much. Now more than ever, the Rap is a river that Virginia anglers shouldn't miss.

Top: The Army Corps of Engineers blows up the Embry Dam. Removing the dam opened up over a hundred miles of spawning ground for stripers and shad. Photo by Beau Beasley. **Bottom:** *Thousands of tons of silt and sand washed downstream after the breaching of the dam. Photo by King Montgomery.*

Types of Fish
The Rappahannock offers a wide variety of species to pursue. Shad and stripers migrate annually, but anglers may prefer to go after the resident populations of smallmouth bass, bluegill, largemouth bass, perch, carp, or catfish.

Known Hatches & Baitfish
Ants, beetles, crayfish, crickets, damselflies, dragonflies, frogs, hellgrammites, and hoppers, as well as other baitfish and minnows. Many of the minnows you see in the Rappahannock are actually shad fry that live in the river for a year before migrating to the Chesapeake Bay.

Equipment to Use
Rods: 5-8 weight, 8-9 feet in length.
Reels: Standard for most species; large arbor for stripers.
Lines: Primarily weight-forward floating; 200-300 grain sinking line for shad.
Leaders: 3X-5X, 9 feet in length.
Wading: Chest waders are best. Float trips are also an option. Be forewarned: the Rappahannock is dangerous. Anglers die here every year. If you wade, you must use felt-soled shoes to be safe.

Flies to Use
For shad: BH Goldilox #4-8, BH Woolly Bugger #6-10, Bruce's Little Bow #2-6, Crazy Charlie #6-8, Mohnsen's Buggit #6-8, Simmons' Shad Fly #4-6, Super Patuxent Special #6-10, Tommy's Flash Torpedo #4-6, Tommy's Torpedo #4-6.
For smallies and stripers: Bruce's Bay Anchovie #2, Claw-Dad #2-6, Chocklett's Gummy Minnow #6, CK Baitfish #1, Clouser Minnow #1/0-6, Cramer's Jail Bait Minnow #2-4, DuBiel's Finesse Fly #2-4, DuBiel's Lil'hadden #1/0-2, DuBiel's Red-Ducer #1/0-2, Finn's Golden Retriever #6-10, Hansen's Electric Frog #6, Hickey's Condor #6-12, Kreelex #2-6, Lefty's Deceiver #2/0-2, Lefty's Half and Half, #2/0-2, MC2 Crayfish #4-6, Murray's Lead Eye Hellgrammite #6, Murray's Marauder #6, Patuxent Special #6-10, San Antonio Worm #4, Shenk's White Minnow #4-6, Super Patuxent Special #6-10, Tommy's Eel Fly #2/0-1/0, Trow's Minnow #1/0-6, Walt's Popper #2-12.

When to Fish
Open all year.

Season & Limits
For shad and stripers, prime time is the last week of March through the first week of May. A rough rule of thumb is that if the cherry trees are blooming, then shad are in the water. From late May through the end of November, some of the best fishing for warm water fish can be had here.

Nearby Fly Fishing
The Rapidan feeds into the Rappahannock and is a great fishery in its own right. You can also fish the James River, which is only an hour away.

Accommodations & Services
The bulk of the services for the Rappahannock will be found in the city of Fredericksburg.

Rating
The Rap rates an 8.

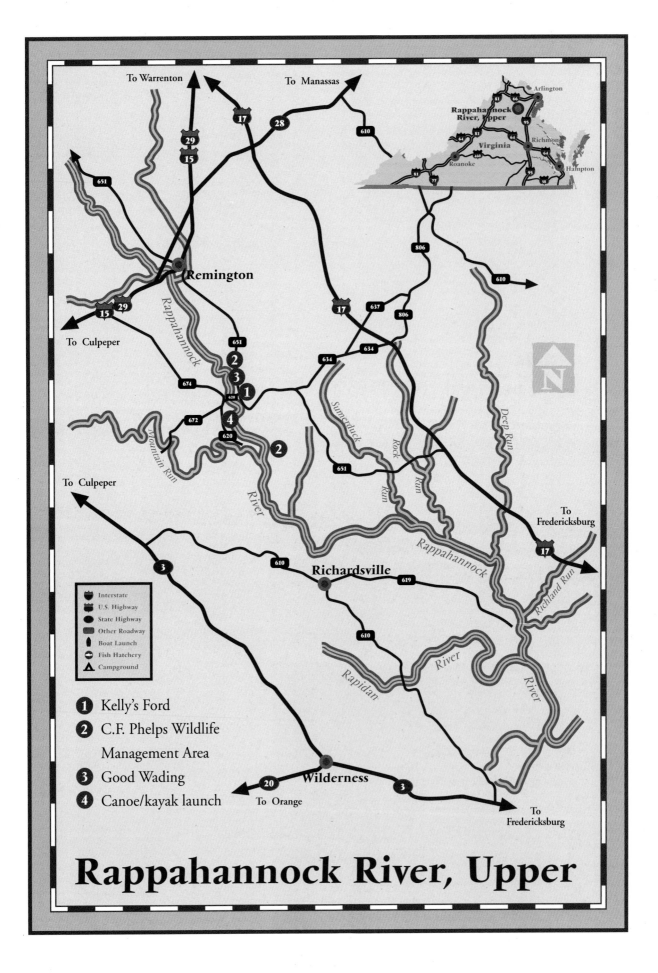

To Warrenton

To Manassas

Rappahannock
River, Upper

Arlington

Virginia

Richmond

Roanoke

Hampton

651

17

28

610

29
15

806

651

610

Remington

Rappahannock

17

637

806

15 29

634

To Culpeper

651

634

2

3

674

1

620

672

4

620

651

Sumerduck

Rock Run

Run

Deep Run

2

River

N

Mountain Run

Rappahannock

To
Fredericksburg

To Culpeper

17

Richland Run

3

610

Richardsville

619

610

Legend

Interstate

U.S. Highway

State Highway

Other Roadway

Boat Launch

Fish Hatchery

Campground

River

Rapidan

River

River

1 Kelly's Ford

2 C.F. Phelps Wildlife
   Management Area

3 Good Wading

4 Canoe/kayak launch

20

Wilderness

3

To Orange

To
Fredericksburg

Rappahannock River, Upper

Rappahannock River
Upper Section

Most Virginia anglers know of the Rappahannock but know little about its upper reaches—which is why I have dedicated a separate section to the upper Rap in this book. Anglers will find access to the water at Kelly's Ford near the small town of Remington. Like so much of the Old Dominion, this area was the site of some bloody Civil War engagements, but one story also speaks to the fact that the war was fought by real *people*—people on opposing sides of the conflict who had had personal relationships before the fighting and who often rekindled those relationships after the war ended. One such relationship existed between Union General William Averell and Confederate General Fitzhugh Lee, who had been classmates together at West Point prior to hostilities.

Lee had taunted Averell throughout the war, leaving notes on trees after engagements and generally casting aspersions on the Union Calvary, which Averell led. In one case Lee left a note for Averell near the Rappahannock that read in part, "If you won't go home, return my visit and bring me back a sack of coffee." Later after the Battle of Brandy Station, the largest cavalry engagement in the Civil War, the Confederate Army beat back the Union Cavalry after many hours of fighting—but the battle had cost them dearly. The powerful Confederate Cavalry

Smallmouth and other fish like the rocky structure of the upper Rappahannock. Photo by King Montgomery.

A view of the river from the C.F. Phelps Wildlife Management Area. Photo by Beau Beasley.

This sunfish fell for a tan Claw-Dad. Photo by Beau Beasley.

The upper Rappahannock is often less pressured than the lower.
Photo by Beau Beasley.

and the near-mythic belief in its invincibility were dealt a heavy blow that day. After the Battle of Brandy Station, Averell left his former roommate a note of his own: "Dear Fitz, here's your coffee. Here's your visit. How do you like it?"

The only reminders you'll find along the Rap of those bloody, raging engagements are a few historical markers. The bridge that crosses over Kelly's Ford provides a good view of the river, both up and downstream. You'll find a boat ramp south of the bridge as well as excellent rock structure and good wading above the bridge at Kelly's Ford. Unfortunately, you might find that some young locals have beaten you to the punch and are using the large pool just above the bridge as a swimming hole. I can assure you that when the kids leave, the fish return.

One of the best access points to the upper Rappahannock is the C. F. Phelps Wildlife Management Area just above Kelly's Ford. Here you'll find a walking trail complete with interpretive history. As you walk the trail toward the river, you'll also find wooden sheds built for handicapped hunters (note the ramps allow wheelchair access). Several areas along the well-maintained trail will eventually lead you alongside the river.

The wildlife area and the upper Rappahannock would be a great place to introduce your children to Virginia's great outdoors. Steeped as it is in history, lined as it is with a lovely and accessible walking trail, and filled as it is with fish, what more could a child ask for than a day on the upper Rappahannock?

Topwater patterns like Hansen's Electric Frog are a great alternative to traditional surface patterns. Photo by King Montgomery.

Types of Fish

Smallmouth bass are the predominant species here, but anglers may also catch shad in the spring once they have moved up past Fredericksburg. Fly anglers can also expect to catch bluegill, ring perch, largemouth, and even the occasional catfish.

Known Hatches

Hatches are consistent with other warm water rivers. Terrestrials like crickets, damselflies, dragonflies, and hoppers are common. Various baitfish and minnows are thick in this river, as well as frogs, crayfish, and hellgrammites.

Equipment to Use

Rods: 6-8 weight, 8-9 feet in length.
Reels: Standard mechanical.
Lines: Weight-forward floating, matched to rod. The occasional sink tip is all you need.
Leaders: 3X-4X leaders, 9 feet in length.
Wading: There is a very good boat and canoe launch at Kelly's Ford as well as good wading. This is the perfect setup for a float down river to fish the small islands and sand bars. Above Kelly's Ford at the C. F. Phelps Wildlife Management Area is an excellent place to wade with plenty of rock structure.

Flies to Use

For shad: Use Mohnsen's Buggit #6-8, Simmons' Shad Fly #4-6, Super Patuxent Special #6-10, Tommy's Flash Torpedo #4-6, Tommy's Torpedo #4-6.
For all other species: Use BH Goldilox #4-8, Bruce's Little Bow #2-6, Claw-Dad #2-6, Chocklett's Disc Slider #1/0, Chocklett's Gummy Minnow #6, Dover's Peach Fly #6-10, CK Baitfish #1, Clouser Minnow #1/0-6, Cramer's Jail Bait Minnow #2-4, Finn's Golden Retriever# 6-10, Hansen's Electric Frog #6, Hickey's Condor #6-12, Kreelex #2-6, MC2 Crayfish #4-6, Murray's Lead Eye Hellgrammite #6, Murray's Marauder #6, Patuxent Special #6-10, San Antonio Worm #4, Shenk's White Minnow #4-6, Super Patuxent Special #6-10, Trow's Minnow #1/0-6, Walt's Popper #2-12.

When to Fish

The upper Rappahannock is open all year. Shad show up here in mid-April with the remainder of the species remaining year-round.

Season & Limits

Anglers often overlook the large smallmouth bass here, searching for lunkers in larger water instead. Keep in mind that bigger water doesn't necessarily mean larger fish.

Nearby Fly Fishing

Your nearest alternative water may be the lower Rapidan near Eley's Ford just prior to Route 3 off Route 610.

Accommodations & Services

The closest large city to the upper reaches of the Rappahannock is still Fredericksburg, but the closest fly shops are The Castaway Company in Culpeper and Rhodes Fly Shop in Warrenton. Numerous historic B&Bs dot the area, so perhaps anglers might consider a weekend getaway.

Rating

The upper Rappahannock rates a 7.

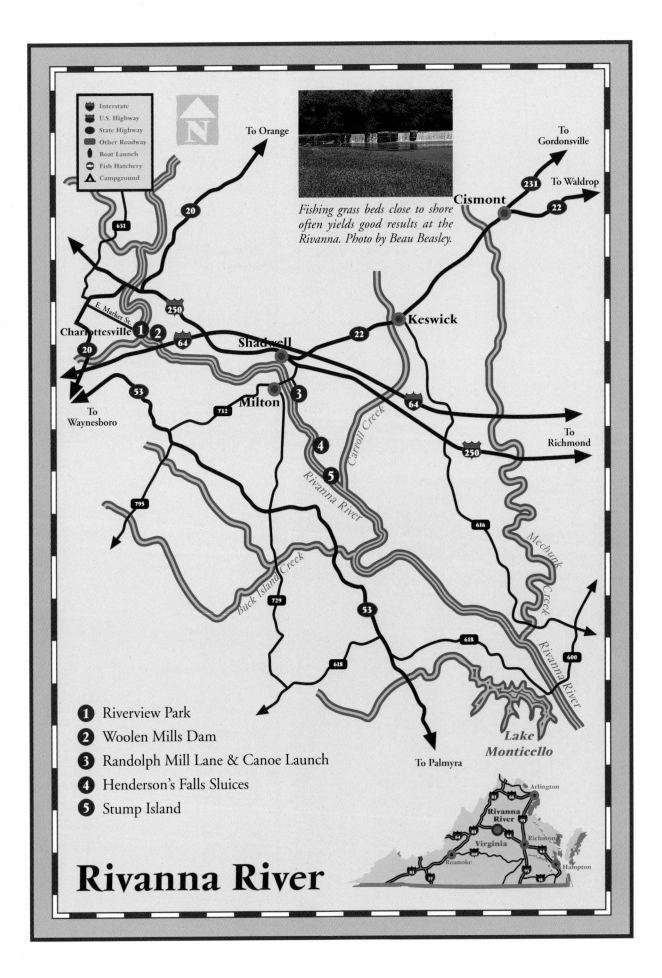

Fishing grass beds close to shore often yields good results at the Rivanna. Photo by Beau Beasley.

To Orange

To Gordonsville

To Waldrop

Cismont

231

22

E. Market St.

Keswick

Charlottesville

Shadwell

22

64

Milton

250

64

To Richmond

To Waynesboro

53

732

Carroll Creek

Rivanna River

To Palmyra

795

Buck Island Creek

729

53

618

Mechunk Creek

616

618

600

Rivanna River

Lake Monticello

1 Riverview Park

2 Woolen Mills Dam

3 Randolph Mill Lane & Canoe Launch

4 Henderson's Falls Sluices

5 Stump Island

Rivanna River

Arlington

Rivanna River

Virginia

Richmond

Roanoke

Hampton

Interstate
U.S. Highway
State Highway
Other Roadway
Boat Launch
Fish Hatchery
Campground

Rivanna River

Occasionally good fly angling rivers simply get overlooked. Such is the case of the Rivanna near Charlottesville. Named after Princess Anne of England, this river has largely been ignored for better-known waters like the Shenandoah and the James. Good access points for wading anglers include a spot near Shadwell off of route 250 and a point near the Woolen Mills Dam.

The Shadwell access point marks a beautiful stretch of the river that anglers may fish either up or downstream with ease. The stretch of river adjacent to the Woolen Mills Dam lacks the ambience of the Shadwell area, but the bass don't seem to mind. The dam was built about 1830 by the Rivanna Navigation Company to power the textile mill and to help bateaux transport goods up and down the river. Remnants of the textile factory can still be seen today, complete with smokestacks. If you fish near the Woolen Mills Dam, don't be put off by the presence of other folks enjoying the river—simply move downstream.

Woolen Mills Dam—the future of which is uncertain— near Charlottesville. Photo by Beau Beasley.

Overhanging trees and excellent rock formations mean great cover for fish on the Rivanna. Photo by Beau Beasley.

The Rivanna—one of Virginia's most underrated fisheries.
Photo by Beau Beasley.

Anglers will find easy wading in much of the Rivanna, and though the fish are not huge they are plentiful, with largemouth and smallmouth bass making up the bulk of the gamefish along with bluegill and the occasional longnose gar. The Rivanna sports two interesting features worth noting: First, anglers will find some very interesting rock formations that provide wonderful pools and structure for fish. Second, a dark green moss grows on much of the Rivanna's bottom, which makes judging its depth difficult. Don't forget to wear polarized sunglasses here, both for sun protection and to enable you to navigate the Rivanna's mossy river bottom with ease.

Gordon English fishing the Rivanna River, with the Woolen Mills smokestack in the background. Photo by Beau Beasley.

Types of Fish
Largemouth bass, smallmouth bass, bluegill, carp and longnose gar.

Known Hatches
Ants, beetles, crayfish, crickets, damselflies, dragonflies, frogs, hellgrammites, and hoppers, as well as various baitfish and minnows.

Equipment to Use
Rods: 5-7 weight, 8-9 feet in length
Reels: Standard.
Lines: Weight-forward floating lines to match rods, with the occasional sink tip.
Leaders: 3X-5X leaders to 9 feet.
Wading: Use chest waders and felt-soled shoes.

Flies to Use
BH Goldilox #4-10, Bruce's Little Bow #6, Chocklett's Disc Slider #2-6, Chocklett's Gummy Minnow #2-6, CK Baitfish #2-6, Clouser Minnow #1/0-6, Claw-Dad #6-8, Cramer's Jail Bait #2-6, Finn's Golden Retriever #6, Hansen's Electric Frog #6, Hickey's Condor #6-12, Kreelex #4-6, MC2 Crayfish #4-6, Murray's Lead Eye Hellgrammite #4-6, Murray's Marauder #4-8, Patuxent Special #6-10, San Antonio Worm #4, Shenk's White Minnow #6-8, Super Patuxent Special #6-10, Trow's The One #2-8, Walt's Poppers #2-12.

When to Fish
Open all year.

Season & Limits
Almost any spring day can be good on the Rivanna, though after late June the water can get low. By early September, however, the water is usually back up, and you can fish through November in a good season.

Nearby Fly Fishing
The James, Rappahannock, and Shenandoah Rivers as well as the Shenandoah National Park are all excellent alternatives.

Accommodations & Services
Anglers will find everything they need—and superior dining and lodging options—in the picturesque and historic city of Charlottesville. The town also boasts two fine fly shops, Albemarle Angler and Mountain River Outdoors.

Rating
The Rivanna may not have the reputation of the nearby James, but it also doesn't have to contend with the same pressure. The Rivanna is a good little river that rates a 6 with me.

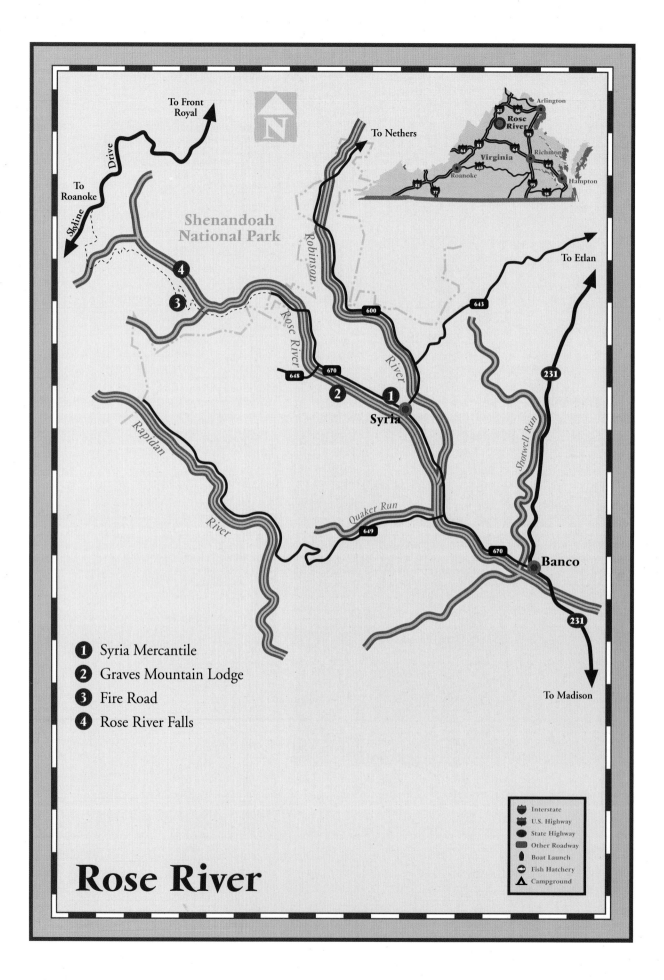

To Front Royal

Skyline Drive

To Roanoke

Shenandoah National Park

To Nethers

Robinson

Rose River

River

To Etlan

648   670

4

3

2   1

Syria

643

231

Shotwell Run

Rapidan

River

Quaker Run

649

670

Banco

231

To Madison

1 Syria Mercantile
2 Graves Mountain Lodge
3 Fire Road
4 Rose River Falls

Arlington
Rose River
Virginia
Richmond
Roanoke
Hampton

Interstate
U.S. Highway
State Highway
Other Roadway
Boat Launch
Fish Hatchery
Campground

Rose River

Rose River

The easiest way to reach the Rose River is to drive to the end of Route 670 and park at the end of the turnout. A sign announces that you are entering the Shenandoah National Park, and a wooden kiosk provides information about the river and the fire trail that traverses the mountainous region and much of this river. This fire road also doubles as a horse trail and hiking path, so don't be surprised to see day trippers sharing the road with you. And on that note, be advised that because you are sharing the road with horses, you should watch your step. Enough said.

Syria Mercantile, a fixture on the outskirts of the park, is a great place to pick up those last minute items you left at the house as you rushed out for a great day of brook trout fishing. Although they don't have much in the way of fly fishing gear, they carry nearly everything else including detailed park maps, clothes, drinks, and snacks. Heck, they even have a post office inside the store. Connie Lynn, a local who has worked at the store

A typical plunge pool on the Rose River. Photo by Beau Beasley.

The Rose River tends to hold a bit more water than some of the other streams in the Shenandoah National Park, making it fishable nearly all year. Photo by Beau Beasley.

Wildlife researchers are constantly monitoring the waters of the Shenandoah National Park. Photo by Beau Beasley.

Future fly angler Andrew Wilson with a mayfly. Photo by Beau Beasley.

for years, will be happy to give you the latest fishing regulations or help you get your bearings if you get lost. If she's not around, ask for assistance from one of the older gentlemen sitting on the front porch. They're accustomed to wayward park visitors.

Graves Mountain Lodge, where Trout Unlimited holds their kids' camp each summer, will be on your left just off of Route 670. At this point you are only a few miles from the Rose, but the road can be rough here so take your time.

The fire trail that flanks the Rose is 100 yards away from the river, so don't expect to see water as soon as you start your walk to the river. As one might expect, the section right next to the parking area gets hit pretty hard. So do yourself a favor and start out with a good walk up into the park to give yourself some better water. My advice is to walk a good 200–300 yards up the trail before you begin fishing. When you feel you've reached an area you want to fish, get off the trail and head for the sound of rushing water. The forest is so thick here that at times the river is completely obscured from the trail. Just listen for the water, and try to walk in as straight a path as you can towards the river.

The Rose has classic plunge pools created by crystal clear water and large boulders that flank the sides of the stream. The good news is that the cover is not quite as tight as it is in other places of the park—you'll actually have room to cast. The bad news is that the water is sometimes quite low, so you won't have much room for your pattern to drift. Your best bet is to approach each pool carefully and watch for rising trout before you cast.

After a heavy rain, many trout anglers avoid small trout streams like the Rose thinking it will be off color and running too high to fish. In fact, the Rose, like most of the other park streams, clears quickly because the stream bed is usually solid rock. The abundance of water a day or two after a downpour might just give you the edge you need to catch these wily fish, which normally spend a great deal of time hiding from predators because the Rose is usually gin clear.

Turn over a rock and check out what's hatching.
Photo by Beau Beasley.

Types of Fish
Rose River anglers will find an eager population of brook trout.

Known Hatches
No big surprises here: expect to see Winter Stoneflies, Blue Quills, Hendricksons, March Browns, Little Yellow Stoneflies, Sulfurs, Quill Gordons, Caddis, Cahills, inchworms, and terrestrials.

Equipment to Use
Rods: 3-4 weight, 7½-8 feet in length.
Reels: Standard mechanical.
Lines: Weight-forward floating, matched to rod.
Leaders: 4X-6X leaders, 9 feet in length.
Wading: Hip waders are fine here.

Flies to Use
Dries: Adams #14-20, BWO #14-20, Braided Butt Damsel #10-12, Dusty's Deviant #12-16, Elk Hair Caddis #14-20, Flying Ant #10-18, Gelso's Little Black Stonefly #16-20, Lt. Cahill #14-20, Little Yellow Sally #14-20, March Brown #10-14, Murray's Mr. Rapidan #14-20, Pale Morning Dun #14-20, Quill Gordon #12-22, Stimulator #12-20, Steeves' Attract Ant #16-20, Steeves' Bark Beetle #16-20, Steeves' Crystal Butt Cricket #8-10.
Nymphs & Streamers: Beadhead Hare's Ear #14-20, Beadhead Prince Nymph #14-20, Coburn's Cress Bug #14-20, Coburn's Inchworm #12-14, Dover's Peach Fly #8-10, Egg #6-20, Green Weenie #14-16, Pheasant Tail #14-20, Scud #10-18, Sculpin #6-8, Woolly Bugger #8-10.

When to Fish
Like most of the trout streams in the Shenandoah National Park, watch for things to really warm up on the Rose toward the end of March. The Rose can fish well all through October if the conditions are right. This stream is open to fishing all year.

Season & Limits
I recommend anglers release any trout caught on the Rose.

Nearby Fly Fishing
Many other brook trout fisheries are nearby, including the Rapidan and the Conway. Anglers who want to go after warm water fish can try the South Fork of the Shenandoah.

Accommodations & Services
The closest thing to a town in this neck of the woods is Sperryville. Pick up flies and other gear at Rhodes Fly Shop in Warrenton or The Castaway Company in Culpeper before you head out to Shenandoah National Park.

Rating
The Rose is a beautiful little stream that rates a 7.

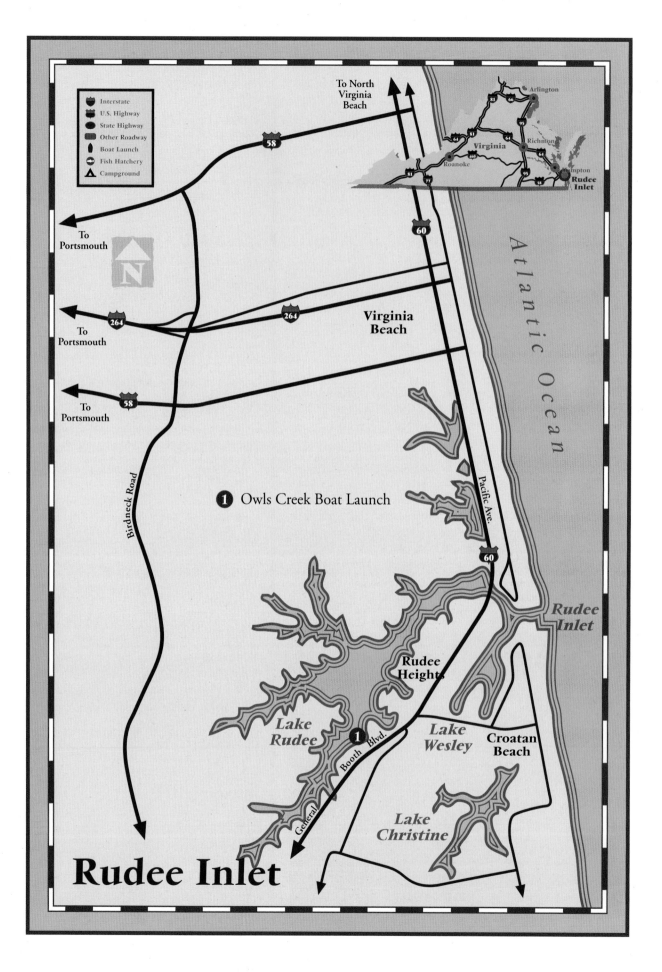

Rudee Inlet

Rudee Inlet

Hard-core saltwater fly anglers are always on the lookout for hotspots and few offer the options of Rudee Inlet in the heart of Virginia Beach. It is just the ticket for anglers in need of a quick saltwater fix. Rudee Inlet, the southernmost inlet before North Carolina, is sort of hiding in the wide open waiting to be discovered. As near as I can tell, only the kayak anglers are making the most of this area—and even they will tell you that it's not being fished to its fullest potential.

Screaming Navy fighter jets roared overhead when I first fished Rudee Inlet, and although at first I found their pronounced presence a bit unnerving, I grew to almost enjoy them. I like to think of it as my tax dollars at work. Wading is not really an option here, so a boat is a must. You'll find a large boat dock as well as bathrooms. Although Rudee Inlet boasts plenty of room for multiple boats, the only other watercraft I saw when I was fishing was another boat in my party. It seems we had the entire inlet to ourselves.

Think of Rudee Inlet as a gigantic saltwater pond with a section that leads directly to the Atlantic Ocean. Because the inlet does open to the ocean, some anglers opt to enter the Bay here—though they soon return if the wind on the Bay gets bad. Like most oceanfront property, you'll see beautiful homes that back up to the shoreline here and anglers have nicknamed the inlet Rich Man's Cove.

Anglers can use a kayak or wade in Rudee Inlet. Photo by Beau Beasley.

Inlets offer anglers and fish protection from the ever-present winds on the Bay. Photo by Melissa Newsome.

The author kneels with a nice drum caught on the fly.
Photo by Steve Probasco.

Rudee Inlet is the perfect place to launch your kayak or canoe and just do a little exploring. You'll find small strips of land in the water, which provide great natural structure for the fish. These areas can hardly be called islands, but they do provide a place for sea grasses to gain a foothold, which of course attract baitfish, which in turn entice the larger fish.

Most Mid-Atlantic anglers know the Chesapeake Bay, but few know the little gem that is Rudee Inlet. This immensely satisfying and fishable hideaway is easy to reach and should be on your radar screen—even if you're not a Navy flyer.

Saltwater fly anglers usually go for stripers and sea trout, but croakers are also a good game fish. Photo by King Montgomery.

Kayaking for fish has become quite popular in Virginia. Photo by Beau Beasley.

Types of Fish
There are lots of saltwater species to choose from in this fishery. The main species is striper and puppy drum however you can also catch flounder, croaker and speckled trout.

Known Baitfish
Rudee Inlet offers small baitfish a break from the wind. Anglers can expect to see menhaden, shrimp, squid, crabs, and a variety of small baitfish.

Equipment to Use
Rods: 6-9 weight, from 9-10 feet in length.
Reels: Mechanical and palm. If you get into larger fish, however, you'll want a reel with a good drag.
Lines: Fast-intermediate lines are the workhorse here. 200-grain sinking lines will also work.
Leaders: 1X-3X, 9 feet in length.
Wading: Use a boat or kayak.

Flies to Use
Bruce's Bay Anchovie #2, Bruce's Crystal Shrimp #1/0, Clouser Minnow #2/0-4, DuBiel's Finesse Fly #2-4, DuBiel's Lil'hadden #1/0-2, DuBiel's Red-Ducer #1/0-2, Lefty's Deceiver #2/0-2, Lefty's Half and Half #2/0-2, Russell's Mussel #1/0-1, Tommy's Crease Fly #2/0-2, Tommy's Eel Fly #2/0-1/0, Trow's Minnow Saltwater #3/0-6.

When to Fish
There is no bad time to fish Rudee Inlet; nevertheless March through November seems to be the best time to go. Some even fish here during the winter months—and if some bluebird days of winter should pop up, by all means go. This area is shallower than the rest of the Bay and as a result can warm up much faster.

Seasons & Limits
Check with local game laws concerning the creel limits of specific species. They often change according to the time of year.

Nearby Fly Fishing
Anglers are only a hop, skip, and a jump from the Chesapeake Bay and the Lynnhaven River.

Accommodations & Services
Virginia Beach has everything you need, including three general tackle shops that provide local flies and a small assortment of fly gear. You will also pass a Bass Pro Shop in Hampton off of Interstate 64 on your way to Virginia Beach. Heck, bring the family, as Virginia Beach is one of the state's premier coastal destinations.

Rating
Rudee Inlet is an easy 7, and at times this area is red hot and can provide a much-needed break from the Bay's winds.

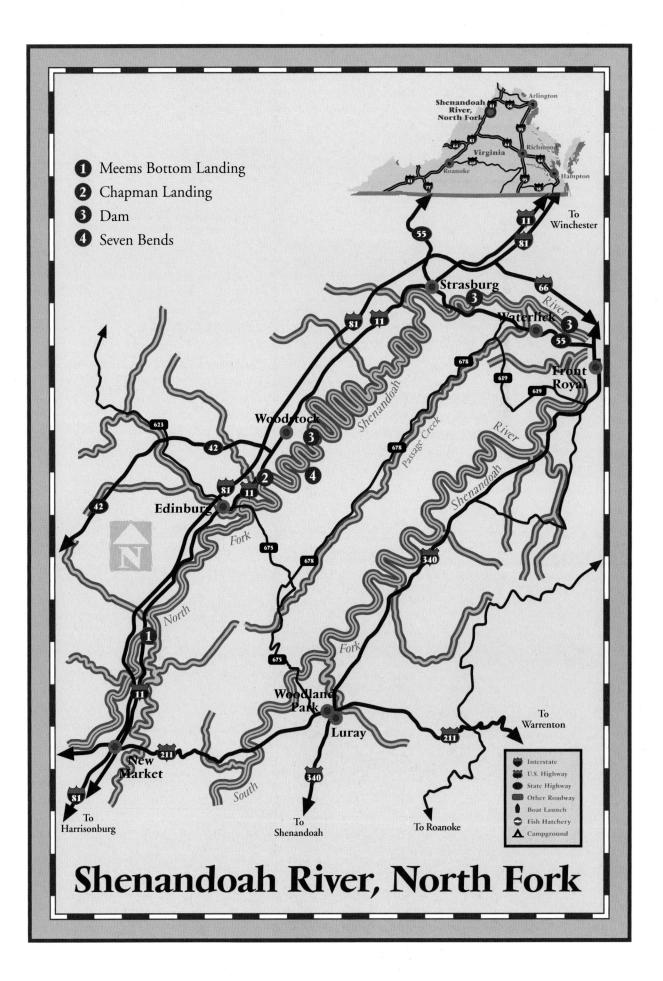

1 Meems Bottom Landing
2 Chapman Landing
3 Dam
4 Seven Bends

Shenandoah River, North Fork

Shenandoah River
North Fork

Less popular than the South Fork, Shenandoah's North Fork is traditionally home to plenty of nice fish. It starts in Rockingham County and snakes its way through the Shenandoah Valley until it meets up with its better-known sister, the South Fork of the Shenandoah, in Front Royal. In between lies over 100 miles of good smallmouth bass water—as well as plenty of solitude, since you'll generally find less fishing pressure on this river.

The North Fork of the Shenandoah has less access and generally less water than the South Fork, which in turn helps keep the fishing and boating pressure at a manageable level. The water can become quite low here in the dead of summer—so much so that canoeists and kayakers often will have to get out of their boats and walk them into deeper water. In some places the North Fork is only the width of a good cast, and really deep water is considered 10-12 feet. Ah, but fly anglers should look at the river differently: what a great opportunity to wade!

I have always admired the North Fork's "seven bends" section near Edinburg. Here the river seems to double back on itself in what appears to be an attempt to confuse anglers

Master carp angler Steve Vlasak with a nice catch.
Photo by Beau Beasley.

Walt Cary has tied Virginia's best-known poppers for nearly 50 years. Walt's Poppers are a must on the Shenandoah. Photo by Beau Beasley.

Choosing the right pattern can make all the difference on the Shenandoah. Photo by King Montgomery.

and boaters. Twisting back and forth in 180-degree turns, it almost seems as though the river can't make up its mind which direction to go. Another interesting set of features are the rock formations that appear under water, which look almost like stair steps running perpendicular to the river's edge. These formations serve anglers as ambush points for small- and largemouth bass and the occasional muskellunge, which dart out from beneath the rock ledges to snag a quick meal.

In addition to low summertime water, you'll find a number of dams on the North Fork: one upstream of Timberville and three more between Edinburg and the Route 758 bridge east of Woodstock. Two much smaller dams are between Strasburg and Riverton. These are not behemoth stone-and-steel structures—the largest dam is near Edinburg and is only 13 feet high.

In 2004, the North Fork of the Shenandoah suffered a tremendous setback: about 80 percent of the smallmouth and sunfish in a 100-mile stretch of the river died. The specific causes of the fish kill remain a mystery, but a complex set of water quality issues is most likely to blame. Nevertheless, the North Fork keeps on a-rollin' and, to paraphrase the song, we anglers love to see it.

The North Fork of the Shenandoah is a good river to wade. Photo by Beau Beasley.

Types of Fish

By and large, Shenandoah anglers are chasing smallies. The North Fork of the Shenandoah, however, also has a good population of sunfish, carp, and rock bass. If you're lucky, you can even get a shot at a muskellunge.

Known Hatches

Ants, beetles, crayfish, crickets, damselflies, dragonflies, frogs, hellgrammites, and hoppers can all be found on the North Fork of the Shenandoah. Madtoms, sculpins, and other various baitfish are common here also.

Equipment to Use

Rods: 3-8 weight, 8-9½ feet in length.
Reels: Standard mechanical.
Lines: Weight-forward floating, matched to rod. The occasional sink tip is advisable.
Leaders: 3X-5X leaders, 9 feet in length.
Wading: Wet wading is one of my favorite ways to explore rivers like the North Fork. For those not so inclined, chest waders will fit the bill (roll them down if it gets too hot).

Flies to Use

BH Goldilox #4-8, Bruce's Little Bow #2-6, Claw-Dad #2-6, Chocklett's Disc Slider #1/0, Chocklett's Gummy Minnow #6, CK Baitfish #1, Clouser Minnow #1/0-6, Cramer's Jail Bait Minnow #2-4, Finn's Golden Retriever #6-10, Hansen's Electric Frog #6, Hickey's Condor #6-12, Kreelex #2-6, MC2 Crayfish #4-6, Murray's Lead Eye Hellgrammite #6, Murray's Marauder #6, Patuxent Special #6-10, San Antonio Worm #4, Shenk's White Minnow #4-6, Super Patuxent Special #6-10, Trow's Minnow #1/0-6, Walt's Popper #2-12.

When to Fish

North Fork Shenandoah fishing is best from March through October, though low water conditions will be a challenge after June.

Season & Limits

Check with local game laws for creel limits.

Nearby Fly Fishing

Alternatives include the South Fork of the Shenandoah as well as Passage Creek and the surrounding Shenandoah National Park.

Accommodations & Services

Edinburg serves as a pleasant base of operations while fishing the North Fork, with B&Bs, restaurants, and Murray's Fly Shop.

Rating

The North Fork is a wonderful river and rates a solid 7.

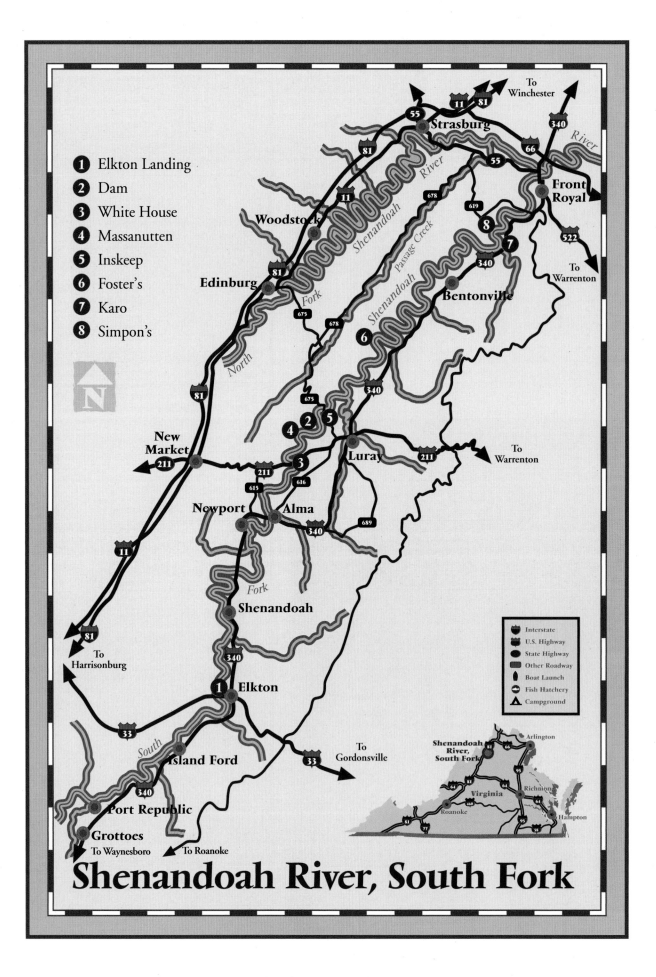

① Elkton Landing
② Dam
③ White House
④ Massanutten
⑤ Inskeep
⑥ Foster's
⑦ Karo
⑧ Simpon's

To Winchester

Strasburg

Front Royal

River

Shenandoah River

Passage Creek

Shenandoah River

Woodstock

Edinburg

North Fork

Bentonville

To Warrenton

⑥

New Market

④ ② ⑤
③
Luray

To Warrenton

Newport Alma

Shenandoah

Fork

To Harrisonburg

① Elkton

South

Island Ford

To Gordonsville

Port Republic

Grottoes
To Waynesboro   To Roanoke

Interstate
U.S. Highway
State Highway
Other Roadway
Boat Launch
Fish Hatchery
Campground

Shenandoah River, South Fork

Shenandoah River, South Fork

Arlington

Virginia   Richmond

Roanoke   Hampton

Shenandoah River, South Fork

Shenandoah River
South Fork

Next to the James, no other river in Virginia is dearer to the smallmouth angler's heart than the Shenandoah. Valley residents have long believed that the river's name means "daughter of the stars"—and the romantic moniker is certainly fitting, even if this water has seen more than its share of floods, droughts, bloody Civil War battles, and, more recently, a major fish kill in 2005, similar to that on the North Fork in 2004, and the mainstream Shenandoah in December 2006. Jointly studying the fish kill are the Virginia Department of Game and Inland Fisheries and the Department of Environmental Quality. They estimate that perhaps 80 percent of the adult smallmouth bass population was destroyed during this kill, the causes of which remain a mystery.

Nevertheless, the Shenandoah still boasts plenty of places where you can wet a line. The South Fork is a big river by Virginia standards—which translates to more habitat and therefore more fish. You'll find canoe rentals alongside the river. This is a good place to break out your kayak as well. Either pay someone to shuttle you, hire a guide, or simply float down the river yourself and paddle back up when you feel that you've gone far enough. Floating the South Fork in a kayak or canoe allows you to fish from your boat or stretch your legs and wade in areas that look good.

Beadhead white Woolly Buggers will catch nearly any freshwater fish. Photo by Beau Beasley.

Bryan Kelly with a brace of smallmouth bass. Photo by Beau Beasley.

Quiet pools are perfect for poppers and other surface water patterns.
Photo by Beau Beasley.

In summer, you are likely to encounter pesky star grass on the South Fork. Yes, it's discouraging to have to remove "salad" from your fly on nearly every cast. To avoid the star grass, consider using a weed guard or casting to the edges of this vegetation.

Surface flies like Walt's Poppers or other topwater patterns are killers here. I remember fishing one day on the Shenandoah when blue damselflies were flitting about. I tied on a Hickey's Condor in blue and caught 22 smallies in a single afternoon on a single fly. I'll admit that the pattern was pretty beaten up at the end of the day, but after catching nearly two dozen fish, I didn't think that I could ask that fly for much more.

Bluegill can grow quite large on the Shenandoah.
Photo by Beau Beasley.

Rafts are a great way to float the Shenandoah. Photo by Beau Beasley.

Types of Fish

By and large, anglers are chasing smallies when they fish the Shenandoah. The South Fork of the Shenandoah also has a healthy population of sunfish, carp, and even crappie. Anglers routinely land some nice largemouth bass here.

Known Hatches

Ants, beetles, crayfish, crickets, damselflies, dragonflies, frogs, hellgrammites, and hoppers call this river home. You'll also find madtoms, sculpins, and other various baitfish and minnows.

Equipment to Use

Rods: 3-8 weight, 8-9½ feet in length.
Reels: Standard mechanical.
Lines: Weight-forward floating matched to rod, and the occasional sink tip.
Leaders: 3X-5X, 9 feet in length.
Wading: Everything from hip waders to chest waders work here—and don't discount wet wading. You'll also find a large variety of floats on the Shenandoah.

Flies to Use

BH Goldilox #4-8, Bruce's Little Bow #2-6, Chocklett's Disc Slider #1/0, Chocklett's Gummy Minnow #6, CK Baitfish #1, Claw-Dad #2-6, Clouser Minnow #1/0-6, Cramer's Jail Bait Minnow #2-4, Finn's Golden Retriever #6-10, Hansen's Electric Frog #6, Hickey's Condor #6-12, Kreelex #2-6, MC2 Crayfish #4-6, Murray's Lead-Eye Hellgrammite #6, Murray's Marauder #6, Patuxent Special #6-10, San Antonio Worm #4, Shenk's White Minnow #4-6, Super Patuxent Special #6-10, Trow's Minnow #1/0-6, Walt's Popper #2-12.

When to Fish

The best fishing takes place between March and October—and can even run into early December if the weather stays warm. May through early July is primetime. You can wade here, but a drift boat or personal watercraft allows you to cover much more water.

Seasons & Limits

Check with local game laws for creel limits.

Nearby Fly Fishing

Other options include the North Fork of the Shenandoah as well as Passage Creek and the surrounding Shenandoah National Park.

Accommodations & Services

The largest cities near the South Fork of the Shenandoah are Harrisonburg and Charlottesville—and both make great jumping-off points. Guides tend to favor picking up clients in the centrally located small town of Luray. If you do go through Luray, don't miss their famous underground caverns. They're spectacular and provide wonder for the whole family. Remember, though, that regardless of the above-ground temperature, the caverns remain a brisk 54 degrees Fahrenheit. Dress accordingly.

The South Fork of the Shenandoah is home to the Shenandoah Riverkeeper Jamboree, which strives to raise awareness for this river. For more information on this important conservation organization, visit www.shenandoahriverkeeper.org.

The closest fly shops include Mossy Creek Fly Fishing and Albemarle Angler, both of which are staffed by knowledgeable guides who fish the river often.

Rating

The South Fork of the Shenandoah handily rates an 8.

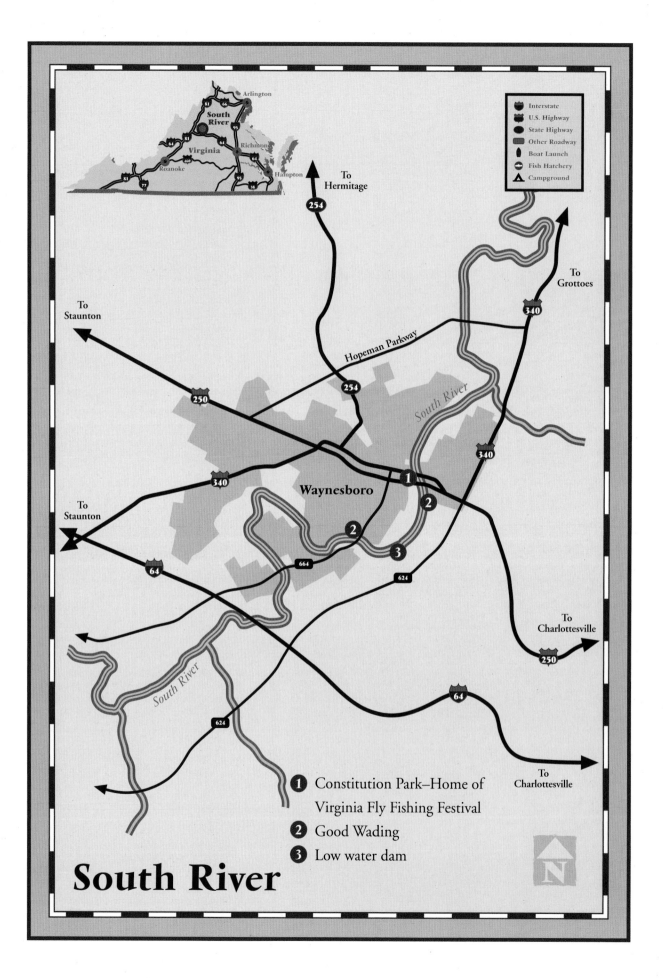

To Hermitage
254

To Grottoes

To Staunton
250

Hopeman Parkway
254

South River
340

To Staunton
340

Waynesboro
1
2
2
3
664
624

64

250
To Charlottesville

64
To Charlottesville

624
South River

Interstate
U.S. Highway
State Highway
Other Roadway
Boat Launch
Fish Hatchery
Campground

1 Constitution Park–Home of
Virginia Fly Fishing Festival

2 Good Wading

3 Low water dam

South River

N

South River

South River is one of the most underrated fisheries in the Old Dominion. Winding first through farmland, the South River gathers steam from feeder creeks and eventually combines with North River to form the South Fork of the Shenandoah. It surprises most anglers to learn that South River was the first urban trout fishery in Virginia and home to the state's first Trout Unlimited chapter.

It should come as no surprise, however, that as an urban trout fishery the river runs right through the middle of downtown Waynesboro. South River has seen its share of abuse in years past. Locals recall the story of how the river actually caught fire one day! Waynesboro residents could tell what color dye the adjacent corduroy plant was using by looking at the color of the water. Happily, tougher environmental regulations marked the end of those days. Today concerned citizens and conservation groups like the Shenandoah Valley chapter of Trout Unlimited are working together to mitigate the effects on the river.

The variety of the fish in the South River is another welcome surprise: The VDGIF stocks the river with rainbows and browns a few times each year, and a healthy population of bass, bluegill, and even carp also call the water home. A delayed-harvest trout section exists in the river, between the Second Street Bridge

Captain Tommy Mattioli enjoys teaching children how to tie flies at the annual Virginia Fly Fishing Festival. Photo by Beau Beasley.

A view of the South River from the Wayne Avenue Bridge. Photo by Beau Beasley.

The South River, which runs through downtown Waynesboro, is one of Virginia's best-known urban trout streams. Photo by Beau Beasley.

upstream to the base of the Rife Loth Dam. Anglers may have to bushwhack their way through some heavy growth along the banks. The easiest section of the South River to access is in downtown Waynesboro's Constitution Park.

In 1999, local businesses dealt a new and very different hand to the South River. Members of the nonprofit Waynesboro Downtown Development Incorporated (WDDI) came up with an unusual plan to promote tourism in town: They decided to host a fly fishing festival. The annual Virginia Fly Fishing Festival is held each year on the banks of the South River in downtown Waynesboro.

Over the years the festival has grown into the largest fly fishing event in the state and each April draws thousands of anglers from as far away as Georgia. Half of all festival profits go to fund conservation work. In 2007 several large boulders were installed in the river to create structure and habitat for local trout. Recently festival organizers established a foundation to help promote the festival and its ongoing work to protect the rivers of Virginia. For more information on the festival foundation or the festival itself, check the resources section of this book or go to their Web site at www.vaflyfishingfestival.org.

Two local residents, Len Poulin and Dana Quillen, have worked tirelessly to promote the festival and the South River. These concerned citizens and committed conservationists deserve our special thanks and appreciation.

WDDI paved the way for a unique collaboration of commercial interests, local government, conservation organizations, and ordinary citizens, and the city and South River are reaping the dividends today.

Conservation grants from the Virginia Fly Fishing Festival Foundation helped pay for these stones, which are excellent structure for the local trout. Photo by Beau Beasley.

Types of Fish
Rainbows and browns make up most of the cold water fish here. The South River is also home to smallmouth bass, largemouth bass, bluegill, and carp.

Known Hatches
Winter Stonefly, Blue Quill, Hendrickson, March Brown, Little Yellow Stonefly, Sulfur, Quill Gordon, Caddis, Cahill, inchworm, and terrestrials. This river also has a wide variety of baitfish as well as crayfish.

Equipment to Use
Rods: 4-7 weight, 7-9 feet in length.
Reels: Palm drive.
Lines: Weight-forward floating lines matched to rod. Sink tips will help in some places.
Leaders: 3X-6X, 9 feet in length.
Wading: Hip boots or chest waders.

Flies to Use
Dries: Adams #14-20, BWO #14-20, Braided Butt Damsel #10-12, Dusty's Deviant #12-16, Elk Hair Caddis #14-20, Flying Ant #10-18, Gelso's Little Black Stonefly #16-20, Lt. Cahill #14-20, Little Yellow Sally #14-20, March Brown #10-14, Murray's Mr. Rapidan #14-20, Pale Morning Dun #14-20, Quill Gordon #12-22, Stimulator #12-20, Steeves' Attract Ant #16-20, Steeves' Bark Beetle #16-20, Steeves' Crystal Butt Cricket #8-10, Steeves' Disc O' Beetle #14, Steeves' UFO #10. *Nymphs & Streamers:* Beadhead Goldilox #6-10, Beadhead Hare's Ear #14-20, Beadhead Prince Nymph #14-20, Bruce's Little Bow #6, Coburn's Cress Bug #14-20, Coburn's Inchworm #12-14, Egg #6-20, Finn's Golden Retriever #6-10, Green Weenie #14-16, Matuka #4-10, Mickey Finn #6-10, MC2 Crayfish #4-6, Muddler Minnow #6-10, Murray's Marauder #6-10, Pheasant Tail #14-20, River Witch #6, Scud #10-18, Sculpin #4-8, Woolly Bugger #6-10.

When to Fish
The South River fishes best from April to mid-June and late September to mid-November.

Season & Limits
There is a delayed-harvest area that runs from the Second St. Bridge up 2.4 miles to the Rife Loth Dam. From October through May, anglers may use only artificial lures and must release all fish. From June through September, general trout regulations are in effect.

Nearby Fly Fishing
St. Mary's River, Mossy Creek, and several streams in the Shenandoah National Park.

Accommodations & Services
Waynesboro has all the dining, lodging, and services you need. I have enjoyed staying at the Iris Inn and the Belle Hearth, two excellent B&Bs. The closest fly shops with guide service are Albemarle Angler in Charlottesville and Mossy Creek Fly Fishing in Harrisonburg. You can also get the local lowdown from Dominion Outdoors in Fishersville.

Rating
No one will confuse the South River with a pristine stream in the Shenandoah National Park. Nevertheless, fishing the South has its benefits. It's easy to reach, full of a variety of fish, and home to the Virginia Fly Fishing Festival. These reasons earn it a 7.

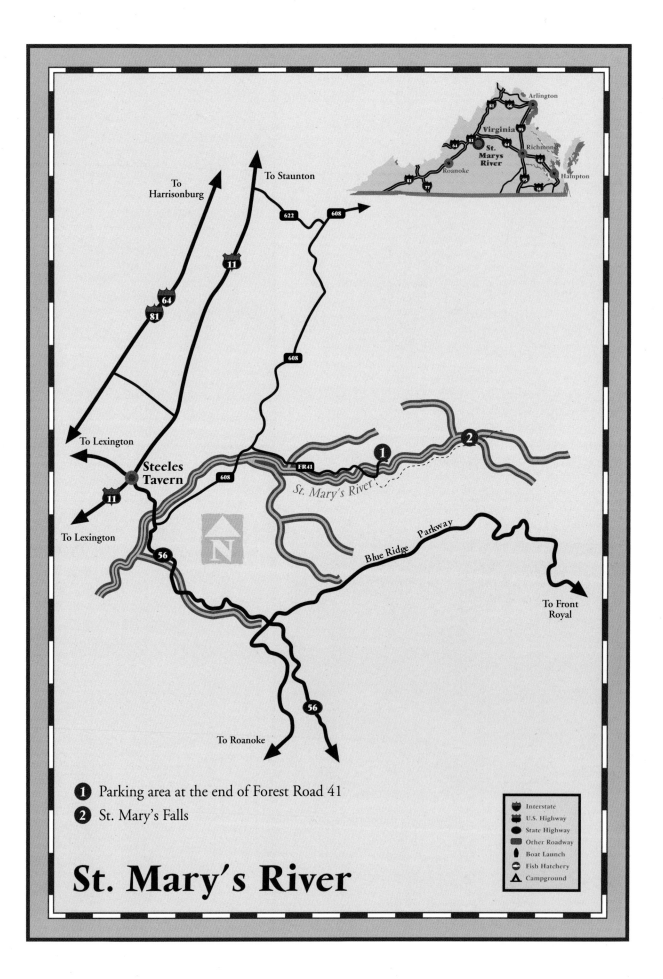

1 Parking area at the end of Forest Road 41

2 St. Mary's Falls

St. Mary's River

St. Mary's River

For decades, anglers after wary mountain trout have enjoyed the St. Mary's River in the heart of Augusta County. Embattled by acid rain in the 1990s, the St. Mary's has made a dramatic turnaround with the help of the U.S. Forest Service, The Fly Fishers of Virginia, and Dominion, a Richmond-based energy company. In 1998 the U.S. Forest Service acted as the lead agency to lime the St. Mary's—no mean feat in this isolated, protected section of the George Washington National Forest. Officials could have brought limestone in by pack mule, but they determined that this river rescue operation would take too long—about six months—and cost far too much. Instead a helicopter dropped crushed limestone into the river, accomplishing the job in a single day. In 2005 officials added more limestone to the St. Mary's River, and although this trout water isn't out of the woods yet, the limestone has certainly improved the current conditions for the fish and thus for anglers and sightseeing hikers.

The St. Mary's is easily accessed off of Fire Road 41—but that's where the easy part ends. Yes, there is a hiking trail that runs along the left side of the river that aids anglers and hikers up the river.

The entrance to the lower portion of the St. Mary's River near Fire Road 41. Photo by Beau Beasley.

An angler fishes just below the waterfall on the upper portion of the St. Mary's. Photo by Dan Genest.

Dead trees and root balls are perfect habitat for trout.
Photo by Beau Beasley.

No doubt this pool holds fish—but they'll be tough to catch, between the gin-clear
water and lack of cover to hide your approach. Photo by Beau Beasley.

Unfortunately this is a double-edged sword: anglers must move farther and farther upstream to find fishable water. There are a few feeder streams that seem to flow into the St. Mary's. They are, however, actually parts of the river itself that have been separated from the main stem, and this can confuse new anglers. In the event that you find yourself disoriented, remember that going downstream leads you back to the parking lot. If you happen to enter the river below the parking lot, you will soon run out onto a main road if you walk far enough.

The St. Mary's River is not for rank beginners and can be intimidating even for the more experienced angler. To begin with, its name is misleading. At first blush, the St. Mary's is much more like a creek than a river, and low water conditions here can make fishing tough. Second, the river can't seem to make up its mind which way it wants to run—sometimes east, sometimes west, sometimes seemingly in both directions simultaneously, branching around small islands that cause you to lose sight of the main river. Third, this constant changing of course is illustrated by the large amounts of stone on each side of the river banks, which make walking up or downstream quite difficult at times. This rock-strewn area is also evidence of a huge amount of water that accompanied Hurricane Isabel in 2003. Finally, the water is gin clear, making a stealthy, cautious approach a must for those who hope to bring the St. Mary's sly mountain trout to hand.

Augusta County boasts some of the best trout fishing in the state—and the St. Mary's may be its crown jewel. Photo by Beau Beasley.

Types of Fish
Mostly brookies, although a few scattered rainbows have been caught here from time to time.

Known Hatches
Winter Stonefly, Quill Gordon, Hendrickson, March Brown, Little Yellow Stonefly, Sulfur, Caddis, Cahill, inchworm, terrestrials, and Slate Drake.

Equipment to Use
Rods: 2-4 weight, 7-8 feet in length.
Reels: Standard.
Lines: Weight-forward floating.
Leaders: 4X-7X tapered from 8-9 feet in length.
Wading: Anglers can get away with hip waders or even just a good pair of felt-soled wading shoes and shorts on the St. Mary's.

Flies to Use
Dries: Adams #14-20, BWO #14-20, Braided Butt Damsel #10-12, Dusty's Deviant #12-16, Elk Hair Caddis #14-20, Flying Ant #10-18, Gelso's Little Black Stonefly #16-20, Lt. Cahill #14-20, Little Yellow Sally #14-20, March Brown #10-14, Murray's Mr. Rapidan #14-20, Pale Morning Dun #14-20, Quill Gordon #12-22, Stimulator #12-20, Steeves' Attract Ant #16-20, Steeves' Bark Beetle #16-20, Steeves' Crystal Butt Cricket #8-10, Steeves' Disc O' Beetle #14, Steeves' UFO #10. *Nymphs & Streamers:* Beadhead Goldilox #6-10, Beadhead Hare's Ear #14-20, Beadhead Prince Nymph #14-20, Coburn's Cress Bug #14-20, Coburn's Inchworm #12-14, Egg #6-20, Finn's Golden Retriever #6-10, Green Weenie #14-16, Matuka #4-10, Mickey Finn #6-10, MC2 Crayfish #4-6, Muddler Minnow #6-10, Pheasant Tail #14-20, River Witch #6, Scud #10-18, Woolly Bugger 6-10.

When to Fish
The best time to fish here is early spring and late fall. And check out the St. Mary's after a good rain. This river clears up much earlier after a downpour than you might expect.

Season & Limits
I encourage all who fish this fragile mountain stream to return anything they catch.

Nearby Fly Fishing
Good fishing can also be found on Mossy Creek, the South River in Waynesboro, and various other rivers in the Shenandoah National Park.

Accommodations & Services
The closest town to the St. Mary's River is Stuart's Draft.

Rating
The St Mary's is well worth a visit, but make no mistake: Anglers are in for quite a hike. For this reason, a trip to the St. Mary's is only for the angler who wants to walk up to fish. With its wild scenery and relatively easy access, the St. Mary's rates a 7.

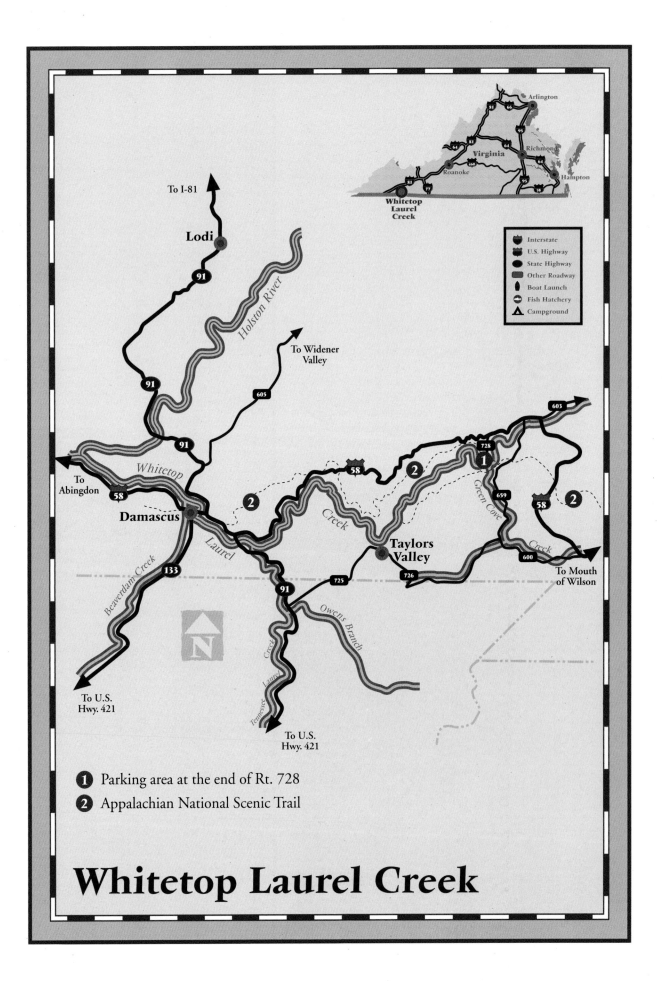

1 Parking area at the end of Rt. 728

2 Appalachian National Scenic Trail

Whitetop Laurel Creek

Whitetop Laurel Creek

One of Virginia's top trout streams, Whitetop Laurel Creek lies in the shadow of Mt. Rogers, the state's highest point. Photo by Beau Beasley.

It would be the rare fly angler indeed who could pass up the opportunity to fish the Whitetop Laurel Creek, which begins on Mount Rogers—the state's highest point—and eventually flows into the Holston River. Long considered some of the best trout water in the state, anglers from across the Old Dominion come here to do battle with the local trout in one of the most picturesque settings in the Mid-Atlantic. Deep in the heart of Washington County, Whitetop Laurel Creek boasts a rare commodity among mountain trout streams—big sky overhead. Here both novice and veteran angler can wet a fly and not worry that every other cast may be gobbled up by a ravenous overhanging river birch.

Long stretches of quiet water and deep, dark pools characterize significant portions of the Whitetop Laurel. Anglers may expect good drifts more than 30 feet long—if crosscurrents don't play games with your pattern. You'll find good cover here; large boulders dot the stream, creating multiple plunge pools suitable for nymphing. Unlike sister stream Big Wilson Creek, the shorelines—and the midstream boulders—at Whitetop

Large plunge pools are the perfect place to fish a nymph. Photo by Beau Beasley.

Unlike most Virginia mountain trout streams, long drifts are possible on Whitetop Laurel Creek. You will, however, still have to contend with cross currents. Photo by Beau Beasley.

Bridges make crossing Whitetop Laurel Creek easy. They also afford anglers the opportunity to scout out the water. Photo by Beau Beasley.

Laurel Creek are much farther apart, so that anglers can get into a desirable casting position fairly easily. A great deal of the river bottom is solid rock, which provides good wading opportunities as well as excellent cover for the resident trout. Whitetop Laurel Creek is also home to some rather large crayfish.

Looking for a river the whole family can enjoy? Whitetop Laurel might be the one, with both the Appalachian Trail and the Virginia Creeper Trail running adjacent to the river in several places. You simply can't beat these hiking trails. Hikers will find bathroom facilities available as well as bear-proof trashcans. For the aesthetically conscious family, beautiful birch trees line the stream along with July-blooming mountain laurel. Numerous wooden observation decks span the river to make casual gazing (and scouting for fish) a breeze. You'll even find places to tie up your horse if your brood prefers getting here on horseback. Not into horses? Consider bringing the mountain bikes and riding the nearby cinder trails. In fact, you might decide to leave the kids behind and bring that mountain bike all by yourself—and use it to put some distance between you and Whitetop Laurel's other angling devotees.

Rainbows and browns make up the lion's share of the trout here, though lucky anglers occasionally catch brook trout. Whitetop Laurel may be your best shot at catching truly wild Virginia rainbows. The trout may not be large—they average 6-8 inches in length, though landing a 17-inch trout here is not unheard of—but catching a wild rainbow in such a beautiful setting makes the trek here worthwhile.

The Virginia Creeper Trail runs adjacent to Whitetop Laurel Creek, making access to the water quite easy. Photo by Beau Beasley.

Types of Fish
Rainbow, brown, and the occasional brook trout.

Known Hatches
Winter Stoneflies, Blue Quills, Hendricksons, March Browns, Little Yellow Stoneflies, Sulfurs, Quill Gordons, Caddis, Cahills, inchworms, terrestrials, and Slate Drakes. I've seen some big crayfish here as well.

Equipment to Use
Rods: 4-6 weight, 7½-8 feet in length.
Reels: Standard mechanical.
Lines: Weight-forward floating, matched to rod.
Leaders: 4X-6X leaders, 9 feet in length.
Wading: Hip waders are fine here, but you'll find some places where chest waders come in mighty handy.

Flies to Use
Dries: Adams #14-20, BWO #14-20, Braided Butt Damsel #10-12, Dusty's Deviant #12-16, Elk Hair Caddis #14-20, Flying Ant #10-18, Gelso's Little Black Stonefly #16-20, Lt. Cahill #14-20, Little Yellow Sally #14-20, March Brown #10-14, Murray's Mr. Rapidan #14-20, Pale Morning Dun #14-20, Quill Gordon #12-22, Stimulator #12-20, Steeves' Attract Ant #16-20, Steeves' Bark Beetle #16-20, Steeves' Crystal Butt Cricket #8-10, Steeves' Disc O' Beetle #14, Steeves' UFO #10.
Nymphs & Streamers: Beadhead Goldilox #6-10, Beadhead Hare's Ear #14-20, Beadhead Prince Nymph #14-20, Bruce's Little Bow #6, Coburn's Cress Bug #14-20, Coburn's Inchworm #12-14, Egg #6-20, Finn's Golden Retriever #6-10, Green Weenie #14-16, Matuka #6-10, Mickey Finn #6-10, MC2 Crayfish #4-6, Muddler Minnow #6-10, Murray's Marauder #6-10, Pheasant Tail #14-20, River Witch #6, Sculpin #6-8, Woolly Bugger #6-10.

When to Fish
Like most mountain trout streams, April through September is prime time. Nevertheless Whitetop Laurel has the potential to fish well through October.

Season & Limits
Open all year. There are two special regulations areas on Whitetop Laurel that limit anglers to single-hook, artificial lures only. Both of these sections are easily seen when walking the river.

Nearby Fly Fishing
Alternative waters include Big Wilson Creek and the South Fork of the Holston River.

Accommodations & Services
The closest town to Whitetop Laurel is tiny Damascus—but don't look for much beyond snacks and gas. The largest nearby population center is Abingdon, home of the Virginia Creeper Fly Shop. Other options include The Orvis Company Store and Blue Ridge Fly Fishers, both in Roanoke.

Rating
Whitetop Laurel rates an 8 on any day. The scenery alone makes it a worthwhile trip.

Private Waters
Catch and Release Only

Escatawba Farms

If you visit Escatawba Farms, you might think that you've died and gone to Montana. But no, you've stumbled into a remote and beautiful corner of the Old Dominion. Escatawba is a Native American word meaning "clear running water," and this is certainly the place to go if your bent runs to stalking big trout in a wild stream setting. Dunlap Creek, which runs through the property, is home to some monster rainbow and browns and is strictly managed as a cold water fishery.

Escatawba Farms can accommodate groups as well as individuals—talk about a breath of fresh air for your next board meeting! Conveniently located near the town of Covington, Dunlap Creek at Escatawba Farms is a wonderful stream that is sure to please.

Contact: Derrick Barr
PO Box 270
Covington, VA 24426
(540) 962-6487
www.escatawba.com

A fly fisher casts into a large pool on Dunlap Creek at Escatawba Farms. Photo by Anthony Vinson Smith.

Greasy Creek Outfitters Trophy Trout Water

Ever had a Virginia trout take you into your backing? Curious to know if your backing is still there? Then I suggest you spend time with Mike Smith of Greasy Creek Outfitters in Carroll County, Virginia.

They access two private stretches of prime trout water that are two miles long and 50 feet wide. These streams provide plenty of room for casting and for trout to take off running. Active trout easily push 20 inches, and anglers often connect with more than one a day. If the bigger fish aren't hungry, you'll have to be content catching lots of 16- to 18-inch trout.

One advantage of this private water is its family-friendly atmosphere. Fly anglers often bring their children along to introduce them to the sport. Make no mistake: This is not fishing in a barrel. The trout scatter all up and down the stream. They hunker down in large pools or hide alongside fallen trees. The denizens of this private water have room to run, and if you hook into one of these beauties, you'll be running, too.

Contact: Greasy Creek Outfitters
5738 Floyd Hwy S
Willis, VA 24380
(540) 789-7811
www.greasycreekoutfitters.com

Big trout like this one often bring about even bigger smiles.

An angler stalking trout on Greasy Creek Outfitters Trophy Trout Waters. Photos courtesy of Greasy Creek Outfitters.

Private Waters
Catch and Release Only

Meadow Lane Lodge

Occasionally you just want to get away from it all. But therein lies the rub: once you've gotten away from it all, you miss the creature comforts of home. Fly anglers who spend the day—or even the week—at Meadow Lane Lodge have found the solution to this problem. The lodge sits on a 1,600-acre farm in historic Bath County—right slap through the middle of which runs Virginia's famed Jackson River. Five generations of the Hirsh Family have lovingly tended to the farm, and thanks to conservation easements, the current Hirshes intend to keep the farm and the river pristine for generations to come. Anglers may fish here for a daily rod rate or for free if they are guests at Meadow Lane Lodge.

Contact: Mrs. Glenn Hirsh
HCR1 Box 110
Warm Springs, VA 24484
(540) 839-5959
www.meadowlanecottages.com

Meadow Lane Lodge offers access to private sections of the Jackson River. Photo courtesy of Meadow Lane Lodge.

Rose River Farm

When Virginia anglers need a get-away-from-it-all, relaxing trout fix, they know where to turn—Rose River Farm. This working farm's owner, Douglas Dear, is a diehard fly angler and has graciously opened his property to anglers who share his trout fishing addiction.

Located in pastoral Madison County and reached from Route 670, it offers easy walking and wading access for anglers of all abilities. Easy fishing access is exactly why Dear, who is the Chairman of the Board for Project Healing Waters, uses his place to host the organization's annual 2-Fly Tournament, which pairs wounded veterans and seasoned guides together each May for a great day on the water.

Its trout look more like steelhead than anything most Virginia anglers see. These are stocked fish but, if you think they're easy to catch, think again. A visit to Rose River Farm is a day well spent.

Contact: Douglas Dear
Rose River Farm
Syria, VA 22743
(703) 759-0186
www.roseriverfarm.com

An angler at Project Healing Waters' annual 2 Fly Contest brings in a nice rainbow. The contest raises thousands of dollars each year for wounded veterans. Photo by Beau Beasley.

Resources

This listing of resources is provided as a courtesy to help you enjoy your travels and fishing experience and is not intended to imply an endorsement of services either by the publisher or author. These listings are as accurate as possible as of the time of publication and are subject to change.

Stores

Albemarle Angler
1129 Emmet St.
Charlottesville, VA 22903
(434) 977-6882
www.albemarleangler.com

Angler's Lane
Graves Mill Center
PO Box 1265
Forest, VA 24551
(434) 385-0200
www.anglerslane.com

Bass Pro Shops
11550 Lakeridge Pkwy.
Ashland, VA 23005
(804) 496-4700
www.basspro.com

Bass Pro Shops
1972 Power Plant Pkwy.
Hampton, VA 23666
(757) 262-5200
www.basspro.com

Crab Creek Outfitters
3584 E. Stratford
Virginia Beach, VA 23455
(757) 464-9190

Dance's Sporting Goods
570 Southpark Blvd.
Colonial Heights, VA 23834
(804) 526-8399
www.dancessportinggoods.net

Dawson's Small Arms
14510 Jefferson Davis Hwy.
Woodbridge, VA 22191
(703) 490-3308

Dominion Outdoors
15 Angela Court
Fishersville, VA 22939
(540) 337-9218
www.dominionoutdoors.com

Gander Mountain #340
3708 Plank Rd.
Fredericksburg, VA 22407
(540) 548-1330
www.gandermountain.com

Gander Mountain #341
10150 Lakeridge Pkwy.
Ashland, VA 23005
(804) 550-2414
www.gandermountain.com

Gander Mountain #342
251 Commonwealth Ct.
Winchester, VA 22602
(540) 868-9312
www.gandermountain.com

Gander Mountain #343
8195 Gander Way
Roanoke, VA 24019
(540) 362-3658
www.gandermountain.com

Greasy Creek Outfitters
5738 Floyd Hwy S
Willis, VA 24380
(540) 789-7811
www.greasycreekoutfitters.com

Green Top Sporting Goods
10193 Washington Hwy.
Glen Allen, VA 23059
(804) 550-2188
www.greentophuntfish.com

The Homestead Resort/ Allegheny Outfitters
1766 Homestead Drive
Hot Springs, VA 24445
(800) 838-1766
www.thehomestead.com

L.L. Bean
8095 Tysons Corner Ctr.
McLean, VA 22102
(703) 288-4466
www.llbean.com

Long Bay Pointe Bait & Tackle
2109 W. Great Neck Rd.
Virginia Beach, VA 23451
(757) 481-7517

Mossy Creek Fly Fishing
2035 East Market St.,
Suite 71-A
Harrisonburg, VA 22801
(540) 434-2444
www.mossycreekflyfishing.com

Mountain Sports, LTD.
1021 Commonwealth Ave.
Bristol, VA 24201
(276) 466-8988
www.mountainsportsltd.com

Murray's Fly Shop
121 Main St.
Edinburg, VA 22824
(540) 984-4212
www.murraysflyshop.com

Orvis Arlington
2879 Clarendon Blvd.
Arlington, VA 22201
(703) 465-0004
www.orvis.com

Orvis Richmond
Short Pump Town Center
11800 West Broad St.,
Suite 1650
Richmond, VA 23233
(804) 253-9000
www.orvis.com

Orvis Roanoke
19 Campbell Ave. SE
Market Square
Roanoke, VA 24011
(540) 345-3635
www.orvis.com

Orvis Tysons Corner
8334-A Leesburg Pike
Vienna, VA 22182
(703) 556-8634
www.orvis.com

Paint Bank General Store
Rt 1 Box 64
Paint Bank, VA 24131
(540) 897-5000
www.paintbankgeneralstore.com

Rhodes Fly Shop
77 Main St.
Warrenton, VA 20186
(540) 347-4162

Severn Wharf Custom Rods
8109 Yacht Haven Rd.
Gloucester Point, VA 23062
(804) 642-0404

A beautiful section of Big Wilson Creek. Photo by Beau Beasley.

Urban Angler, Ltd.
2165 N. Glede Rd.
Arlington, VA 22207
(703) 527-2524
www.urbanangler.com

Virginia Creeper Fly Shop
16501 JEB Stuart Hwy.
Abingdon, VA 24211
(276) 628-3826
www.vcflyshop.com

Guides

Addictive Fly Fishing
George Hughes
3316 Barbour Dr.
Virginia Beach, VA 23456
(757) 589-5945
www.addictiveflyfishing.com

The Angler's Inn
Bryan Kelly
867 W. Washington St.
Harpers Ferry, WV 25425
(304) 535-1239
www.theanglersinn.com

Bay Fly Fishing
Captain Chris Newsome
8090 Kitchener Dr.
Gloucester, VA 23061
(804) 815-4895
www.bayflyfishing.com

Cape Henry Charters
Captain Mike Marsala
624 Cardamon Dr.
Virginia Beach, VA 23464
(757) 724-6453

Bob Cramer Guide Service
9546 Union Springs Rd.
Dayton, VA 22821
(540) 867-9310

Eastern Trophies Fly Fishing
6177 Tag Ct.
Woodbridge, VA 22193
(571) 213-2570
www.easterntrophies.com

Jim Finn's Guide Service
40 Pine Ridge Lane
Mt. Solon, VA 22843
(540) 350-4828
www.mossycreek.com

First Light Outfitters
Demian Wiles
PO Box 270
Covington, VA 24426
(304) 647-2011
(540) 962-6487

Fish the Valley Guide Service
Laurence Eaton
304 Massie St.
Lexington, VA 24450
(540) 460-1786
www.fishthevalley.com

Greasy Creek Outfitters
Mike Smith
PO Box 211
Willis, VA 24380
(540) 789-7811
www.greasycreekoutfitters.com

Hanover Fly Fishers
Harry Robertson
Box 525
Hanover, VA 23069
(804) 537-5036
www.hanoverfly.com

Hatch Matcher Guide Service
L.E. Rhodes
7456 Blenheim Rd.
Scottsville, VA 24590
(434) 286-3366

Dale Huggins
11800 West Broad St.,
Suite 1650
Richmond, VA 23233
(804) 253-9000

Chuck Kraft's Guide Service
2305 Dellmead Lane
Charlottesville, VA 22901
(434) 293-9305

Latitudes Charters
Captain Tony Harding
PO Box 84
Spotsylvania, VA 22553
(540) 582-6396
www.flyfishtidalva.com

Matty-J-Charter Service
Captain Tommy Mattioli
2805 Sandy Bluff Ct.
Richmond, VA 23233
(804) 314-2672
www.matty-j.com

Mountain Trout Outfitters
Chubby Dameron
352 Minor Ridge Rd.
Charlottesville, VA 22901
(434) 531-6938

Ms. Guided
Kiki Galvin
2004 Dexter Dr.
Falls Church, VA 22043
(703) 893-7020
www.msguidedflyfishing.net

New Angle Fishing Adventures
Blane Chocklett
790 Dawnbridge Lane
Troutville, VA 24175
(540) 354-1774

New River Angler
Tom Maynard
218 Wabash Rd.
Staffordsville, VA 24167
(540) 921-4407
www.newriverangler.com

The Outdoorsman
Marcia and Hank Woolman
3085 Burland Lane
The Plains, VA 20198
(540) 253-5545
www.woolmancane.com

Potts Creek Outfitters
Josh Duncan
Route 311
Paint Bank, VA 24131
(540) 897-5555
www.pottscreekoutfitters.com

The Rebel Fly
Captain Russ Cress
10301 Dakins Dr.
Richmond, VA 23236
(804) 543-4368
www.rebelfly.com

Ruthless Fishing
Captain Cory Routh
1425 Preserve Dr.
Virginia Beach, VA 23451
(757) 403-0734
www.ruthlessfishing.com

Speckulater Charters
Capt. Ed Lawrence
P.O. Box 262
Gloucester, VA 23061
(804) 693-5673
www.speckulatercharters.com

Surfside Charter Service
Glenn and Ronnie Sides
3102 Lifsey Ln.
Chesterfield, VA 23832
(804) 405-2977
www.surfsides.com

Tangent Outfitters
Shawn Hash
201 Cascade Dr.
Pembroke, VA 24136
(540) 626-4567
www.newrivertrail.com

Rhea Topping's Mayfly Adventures
9404 Patrick Lane
Upperville, VA 20184
(540) 592-3006
www.rheatopping.com

Two Dogs Trading Company, LLC
Tom Sadler
179 Bald Rock Road
Verona, VA 24482
(202) 957-4748
www.tdtc.biz

Wild Mountain Trout Fly-Fishing
Steve Gibson
409 Yount Ave.
Staunton, VA 24401
(540) 294-0354
www.vaflyfishmtguide.com

Dusty Wissmath Fly Fishing
18116 Raven Rocks Rd.
Bluemont, VA 20135
(540) 554-2676
www.dwflyfishingschool.com

Conservation Groups & Clubs

Chesapeake Bay Foundation—Virginia Chapter
Capitol Place
1108 East Main Street
Suite 1600
Richmond, VA 23219-3539
(804) 780-1392
www.cbf.org

Coastal Conservation Association Virginia
12642 Broad Street Road, Suite A
Richmond, VA 23233
(804) 347-7858
www.ccavirginia.org

Eastern Blue Ridge Fly Fishers
PO Box 1047
Culpeper, VA 22701
www.ebrff.org

Falmouth Flats Fly Fishers
PO Box 8462
Fredericksburg, VA 22401
www.ffflyfishers.org

Fly Fishers of Virginia
P.O. Box 29477
Richmond, VA 23242
(804) 527-1698
www.flyfishersofvirginia.org

Shenandoah River Keeper
Jeff Kelble
PO Box 405
Boyce, VA 22620
(540) 837-1479
jeff@shenandoahriverkeeper.org
www.shenandoahriverkeeper.org

Tidal Potomac Fly Rodders
tidal-potomac-fly-rodders@googlegroups.com
daniel.davala@gmail.com

Kids learning to cast at Graves Mountain Lodge.
Photo by Paul Kearney.

Young anglers attending Trout Unlimited's Fly Fishing Camp look for insects while seining in the Rose River. Photo by Paul Kearney.

Trout Unlimited Conservation and Fishing Camp
Paul Kearney
28 Broad Run Rd.
Browntown, VA 22610
(540)-229-0563
pkearney@crosslink.net
www.tucamp.org

Virginia Coastal Fly Anglers
P.O. Box 2866
Virginia Beach, VA 23450
www.vcfa.org

Virginia Department of Game and Inland Fisheries
4010 West Broad St.
Richmond, VA 23230
(804) 367-1000
www.dgif.virginia.gov

Virginia Fly Fishing Festival
421 West Main St.
Waynesboro, VA 22980
(540) 943-8375
www.vaflyfishingfestival.org

Trout Unlimited Chapters in Virginia

Blacksburg, VA
New River Chapter

Bluefield, VA / WV
Bluefield Chapter

Charlottesville, VA
Thomas Jefferson Chapter

Fairfax, VA
Northern Virginia Chapter

Front Royal, VA
Northern Shenandoah Valley Chapter

Harrisonburg, VA
Massanutten Chapter

Martinsville, VA
Smith River Chapter

Norfolk, VA
Southeast VA Chapter

Richmond, VA
Virginia Capital Chapter

Roanoke, VA
Roanoke Valley Chapter

Warrenton, VA
Rapidan Chapter

Waynesboro, VA
Shenandoah Valley Chapter

Winchester, VA
Winchester Chapter

Wise, VA
Cumberland Mountain Chapter

Conservation

No Nonsense Fly Fishing Guidebooks believes that, in addition to local information and gear, fly fishers need clean water and healthy fish. We encourage preservation, improvement, conservation, enjoyment and understanding of our waters and their inhabitants. While fly fishing, take care of the place, practice catch and release and try to avoid spawning fish.

When you aren't fly fishing, a good way to help all things wild and aquatic is to support organizations dedicated to these ideas. We encourage you to get involved, learn more and to join such organizations.

American Fly Fishing Trade Association .... (706) 355-3804
American Rivers .... (202) 347-7550
Chesapeake Bay Foundation—VA Chapter .... (804) 780-1392
Coastal Conservation Association Virginia .... (804) 347-7858
Federation of Fly Fishers... (406) 222-9369
International Game Fish Association .... (954) 927-2628
International Women Fly Fishers... (925) 934-2461
Mason-Dixon Outdoor Writers Association .... (703) 425-0849
Outdoor Writers Association of America .... (406) 728-7434
Rails-to-Trails Conservancy .... (202) 331-9696
Recreational Fishing Alliance.. (888) JOIN-RFA
Theodore Roosevelt Conservation Partnership .... (877) 770-8722
Trout Unlimited.. (800) 834-2419

Find Your Way with These No Nonsense Guides

Fly Fishing Arizona
Glenn Tinnin
Desert, forest, lava fields, red rocks and canyons. Here is where to go and how to fish 32 cold and warm water streams, lakes, and reservoirs in Arizona.
ISBN 978-1-892469-02-1 .... $19.95

Fly Fishing Southern Baja
Gary Graham
With this book you can fly to Baja, rent a car and go out on your own to find exciting saltwater fly fishing! Mexico's Baja Peninsula is now one of the premier destinations for saltwater fly anglers.
ISBN 978-1-892469-00-7 .... $18.95

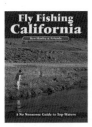

Fly Fishing California
Ken Hanley
Ken Hanley's vast experience gives you a clear understanding of the best places to fish across California—from the Baja coast to the northern wilderness. The redesigned and expanded version of Hanley's popular *Guide to Fly Fishing in Northern California*.
ISBN 978-1-892469-10-6 .... $28.95

Fly Fishing the California Delta
Captain Mike Costello
The first major book describing the techniques for landing trophy striped bass and other species in the California Delta. Covers more than 2,000 levees and 1,200 miles of rivers. In full color and hardcover. 2009
ISBN 978-1-892469-23-6 .... $49.95

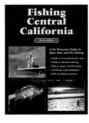

Fishing Central California
Brian Milne
This comprehensive and entertaining guide will improve your chances when you cast a line in Central California and beyond. You'll learn where the best spots are on the streams, rivers, lakes, and ocean fisheries, how to change tactics, and select the right baits, lures, and equipment. Full color.
ISBN 978-1-892469-18-2...........$24.95

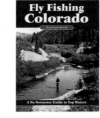

Fly Fishing Colorado
Jackson Streit
Your experienced guide gives you a quick, clear understanding of the information you'll need to fly fish Colorado's most outstanding waters. Use this book to plan your Colorado fly fishing trip, and take it along for ready reference. Full color.
ISBN 978-1-892469-13-7 .... $19.95

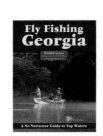

Fly Fishing Georgia
David Cannon
The first and only guide to cover the entire state of Georgia's fly-fishing waters. Details top cold water streams, warm water rivers and impoundments, and coastal saltwater fishing. 29 of the 37 waters featured are within a two-hour drive of the Altanta airport. Full color. 2009
ISBN 978-1-892469-20-5.......... $28.95

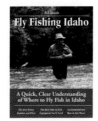

Fly Fishing Idaho
Bill Mason
The Henry's Fork, Salmon, Snake and Silver Creek plus 24 other waters. Bill Mason shares his 30 plus years of Idaho fly fishing. Newly revised.
ISBN 978-1-892469-17-5 .... $18.95

Kayak Fishing
Cory Routh
Routh covers everything you need for safe, fun, and successful kayak fishing. This guide gives you a quick, clear understanding of the essential information you will need to get started in this growing sport. Full color.
ISBN 978-1-892469-19-9 .... $24.95

Fly Fishing Lees Ferry
Dave Foster
This guide provides a clear understanding of the complex and fascinating river that can provide fly anglers 40-fish days. Detailed maps show fly and spin fishing access. Learn about history, boating, and geology. Indispensable for the angler and intrepid visitor to the Marble Canyon.
ISBN 978-1-892469-15-1 .... $18.95

Fly Fishing Magdalena Bay
Gary Graham

Guide and excursion leader Gary Graham (*Baja On The Fly*) lays out the truth about fly fishing for snook in mangroves, and offshore marlin. Photos, illustrations, maps, and travel information, this is "the Bible" for this unique region.
ISBN 978-1-892469-08-3 .... $24.95

Fly Fishing Central & Southeastern Oregon
Harry Teel

New waters, maps, hatch charts and illustrations. The best fly fishing in this popular region. Full color.
ISBN 978-1-892469-09-0 .... $19.95

Seasons of the Metolius
John Judy

This book describes how a beautiful riparian environment both changes and stays the same over the years. Mr. Judy makes his living in nature and chronicles his 30 years of study, writing, and fly fishing his beloved home water, the crystal clear Metolius River in central Oregon.
ISBN 978-1-892469-11-3 .... $20.95

Fly Fishing Pyramid Lake
Terry Barron

The Gem of the Desert is full of huge Lahontan Cutthroat trout. Terry has recorded everything you need to fly fish the most outstanding trophy cutthroat fishery in the U.S. Where else can you get tired of catching 18–25" trout?
ISBN 978-0-9637256-3-9 .... $15.95

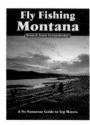

Fly Fishing Montana
Brian & Jenny Grossenbacher

Explore Montana—a fly angler's mecca—as Brian and Jenny Grossenbacher guide you through their beautiful home state. You'll get the information you need to fly fish Montana's outstanding waters.
ISBN 978-1-892469-14-4 .... $28.95

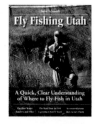

Fly Fishing Utah
Steve Schmidt

Utah yields extraordinary, uncrowded and little known fishing. Steve Schmidt, outfitter and owner of Western Rivers Fly Shop in Salt Lake City has explored these waters for over 28 years. Covers mountain streams and lakes, tailwaters, and reservoirs.
ISBN 978-0-9637256-8-4 .... $19.95

Fly Fishing Nevada
Dave Stanley

The Truckee, Walker, Carson, Eagle, Davis, Ruby, mountain lakes and more. Mr. Stanley is recognized nationwide as the most knowledgeable fly fisher and outdoorsman in the state of Nevada. He owns and operates the Reno Fly Shop and Truckee River Outfitters in Truckee, California.
ISBN 978-0-9637256-2-2 .... $18.95

Business Traveler's Guide To Fly Fishing in the Western States
Bob Zeller

A seasoned road warrior reveals where one can fly fish within a two-hour drive of every major airport in thirteen western states.
ISBN 978-1-892469-01-4 .... $18.95

Fly Fishing New Mexico
Taylor Streit

Since 1970, Mr. Streit has been New Mexico's foremost fly fishing authority and professional guide. He owned the Taos Fly Shop for ten years and managed a bone fishing lodge in the Bahamas. Taylor makes winter fly fishing pilgrimages to Argentina where he escorts fly fishers and explorers.
ISBN 978-1-892469-04-5 .... $19.95

A Woman's Guide To Fly Fishing Favorite Waters
Yvonne Graham

Forty-five of the top women fly fishing experts reveal their favorite waters. From spring creeks in the East, trout waters in the Rockies to exciting Baja: all from the female perspective.
ISBN 978-1-892469-03-8 .... $19.95

Fly Fishing Knots

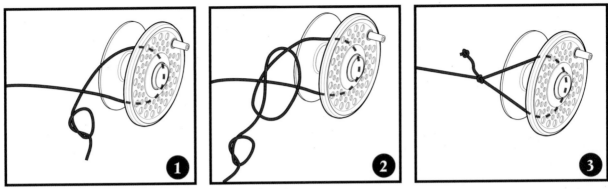

Arbor Knot: *Use this knot to attach backing to your fly reel.*

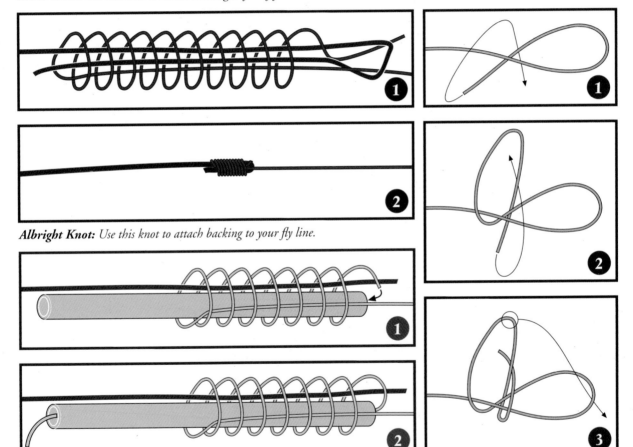

Albright Knot: *Use this knot to attach backing to your fly line.*

Fly Line

Leader

Nail Knot: *Use a nail, needle or a tube to tie this knot, which connects the forward end of the fly line to the butt end of the leader. Follow this with a Perfection Loop and you've got a permanent end loop that allows easy leader changes.*

Perfection Loop: *Use this knot to create a loop in the butt end of the leader for loop-to-loop connections.*